Cover design by Tank Malinowski

Book design by Kimberly Hoyt Willard

Gwen-Marie contact information:
Gwen.Marie@ymail.com

Printed in the United States of America

First Printing: June 2011

Second Printing: September 2012

ISBN- 978-0-557-55079-1

This book is dedicated to angels who have strengthened my wings with love or with fire. There is an angel in each of us, we don't all fly high and we don't all fly fast. Love is the wind that lifts our wings, so love just love.

❖ J.C. ... My best friend

❖ To an angel who works with my husband who gave him an article about a man who felt just like me. I've wanted to write for years. This article said the best therapy to know why you are who you are is to write your life. So thank you.

❖ The Women of Faith Team. Their books, songs and seminars have touched my heart. You are all fly.

❖ Friends like sisters help me fly when I can't; you know who you are. My typing angel who joyfully has flown with me in this writing journey. Love you.

❖ A policeman, helicopter dude, doctors, nurses who the Lord sent to help heal my wings. So much I can't remember...so much I will never forget.

❖ If we are to be judged by our fruit and if my children represent my fruit, I believe I will hear "well done". My husband, Douglas, who has made me possibly the most patient woman ever; always larger than life.

❖ My father, who showed me that I could be loved unconditionally. My mother who is why I learned to fly young. I miss you both.

Some names have been withheld to protect unidentified Idiots, although I love you all

(Angels, it's okay to laugh)

Welcome to My Trip. Sharing this with you took a long time. I can say with confidence this book represents a new beginning of my journey. It's time for me to do the things I put off.

I have been using the phrase "life is a trip" since I was young. The trip may be bizarre, sometimes tragic, sometimes exciting. It is none-the-less, a journey. What we make of the trip and what it makes of us is what makes the journey uniquely yours. It's a bumpy, rocky, draining but exhilarating flight. I refer to all of you as angels 'cuz it's the only way I can pray for each of you not knowing your names. Try to remember our wings are on the inside, like faith...they cannot be seen. Hang on tight as we fly through my trip.

As I have come to the middle of my journey there is even a difference between day and night travel. When you need directions or assistance and have the wisdom to know you need it and the courage to ask, it helps. It could be the guy at the gas station, your hair dresser, a teacher, a friend, your brother or sister, or one of your children that becomes an angel to change one Moment of your life. Living together on this earth, we have common ground, even though we are each made so unique that it doesn't always feel that way. I would like to welcome you on a trip that the Lord made personally mine. We will have things in common and some bumps will be foreign to you. It has been a time of mountains and valleys, slips and slides and learning to balance the terrain. You will meet angels that have saved me from myself and demons that have been overcome. Hopefully it will help you learn perseverance through the trials and celebration of the victories.

When you think you know *who* you are and *what* you are about, one Moment can change your journey. Being in the middle of my life, I thought I'd had quite a few until this past year. My husband and I are both recovering from a motorcycle accident we were in 7 months ago, "coincidentally" as I begin writing. The doctors originally told me I would need at least two years of recovery for the injuries I received. They tell me now that I am miraculously healing. This accident has changed my trip.

So, travel with me as it helps me to remember why I am who I am, and on the way, hopefully, helping you in some small way with your trip. So travel on to understand why I call my life a trip. Hopefully, I can be your angel for a Moment...

Fly On...

FIRST MEMORIES

My first memory is from when I was about four years old. I was brought in a "50 years and older" trailer park until I was five years old. So, to explain a little about this trailer park, my father still worked, but I don't remember anyone else working. There were no children except grandkids that came to visit. My best friend was Mr. Nelsen who was about eighty. I spent a lot of time in his trailer with him. Mr. Nelsen never had any children, so it was just him. The trailer right next to us was Aunt Cecil and Uncle Charlie. As I look back and remember, they were probably about sixty years old. These three people, beside my parents, were the most important people in my life, along with my brother, Arthur, who was thirteen years older than me. As a little girl, I thought I would grow up to marry him.

My first clear memory is sitting with Mr. Nelsen when something came on TV. Within a short period of time, you could hear the whole trailer park crying. I asked him what was wrong, and he said, "Let's give you some ice cream". Mr. Nelsen was so upset he told me that I should go see my Mom, so I went walking home and I could hear everybody crying. I walked in my door and my Mom was sitting on the floor crying. Daddy wasn't home, 'cuz he was never home. I sat down next to my Mom and asked her what was wrong, and she said our President had gotten shot today. I remember her putting her arm around me and I still didn't really understand. I said to her, "Do we know him?" She explained to me what it meant. Even being four years old, I remember thinking that I should be crying too. That was on TV for what seemed like a year. I remember going to see Aunt Cecil next door and asking her about it later. She explained it to me, kind of like my Mom did.

I remember going to Mr. Nelsen's house again the next day, just to make sure he was ok. I remember talking to him for a long time that day, and he was still upset, but I felt that he was better. I worried about him even at four years old. It was not long after that my Mom told me that we were going to move. I remember having a sinking feeling that I was going to lose all of my best friends. I saw them every single day so I knew they would miss me too. In the next few months, I had to say many good-byes.

I remember Aunt Cecil and Uncle Charlie taking me to church. I remember her bringing me up to the priest and he said something over me, and I don't remember what it was. I do remember that it was about protection. As I write this, I realize my journey started at that Moment. I didn't know then how much I would need protection, and I didn't understand anything else he said, except that.

Sometime before we moved, I got pneumonia. I don't remember much about that time, except I didn't go to the doctor; the doctor came to us. The doctor, like everyone else in my life was old. As you walked into the trailer, I was right there in the living room, sleeping on the couch with a breathing machine. My brother was 17 at the time, and I remember him bringing me a cotton candy maker; it was the biggest thing in my life. Before I got sick, I had had long, long curly hair but because my temperature got so high, I lost all of my curls. My mother put it in a ponytail and cut it off. So, while I was trying to get better, I remember feeling like I was bald. I remember Daddy coming home from work and seeing me with no hair. He and Mommy had loud words about the hair.

As I got better the first people I remember seeing were Aunt Cecil and Mr. Nelsen. My Mom told me before I left the house that day that I had to say my good-byes.

I was dressed in a pink dress, pink lace socks, white patent leather shoes, white gloves and no hair. I was never ever dirty, like a normal child 'cuz my friends were old. I made my way to Aunt Cecil's. I remember a lot of kissing, hugging and crying. Then I made my way down the street to Mr. Nelsen's, and he was very sick. After I got older, my Mom explained to me that he had pneumonia, and after we moved away, my Mom told me he had died. The day I said good-bye to him was the first time I saw Mr. Nelsen cry. As I look back I realize that this was the beginning of my love and compassion for older people.

As time goes on, we begin to pack up and move to our new house. To put a little clarity into my life, my father ran a Drive-In theater. Actually, he didn't just run it, it was his life. My mother worked there too. So, we moved closer to the Drive-In.

Our new house was the last one on the left on a dead end road. I remember driving down the street the first time, and seeing kids everywhere. I was scared to death. I knew how to be a big girl, but I didn't know how to be a kid. The first kid I remember meeting was Stanley, and then all the other kids in the neighborhood he introduced me to. We had no computers, no video games, cell phones or such. We had bikes, pollywogs, sledding, and just playing outside. There was a swamp at the end of my street near where we lived in the last house on the left (yes, I know it's a movie). I loved that swamp.

My next vivid memories are when my brother got drafted. It was the Vietnam War, and he had a girlfriend. I remember they got married because he was leaving. I was very upset 'cuz I always thought that I would marry him myself, but grew to love his wife. The

11

wedding was small, and he left not long after that. He had to go to boot camp, because he became a Marine. Arthur told me that I could sleep in his bed to keep it warm for him. My mother wore black from the day he left, until he came home.

Every Tuesday was my father's day off. We went out to dinner every Tuesday. Those were the days I remember feeling more comfortable, 'cuz I didn't have to be a kid. I had my "Shirley Temple" and my parents had their Whiskey Sours.

On the weekends, I would go to the Drive-In with Daddy. We would pop popcorn for the concession stand and he started to teach me how to fix junction boxes for the speakers. Back then the speakers went in the car. All the people that worked at the Drive-In were my pals, and, again, much older than I was. I remember my parents having get-togethers in our basement where the bar was. By the time I was eight, I even knew how to make a few drinks. I was the only kid at these get-togethers, but I was in charge of making Screwdrivers, Whiskey Sours, Grasshoppers, and giving them to the right person. Another memory I have of this time, is my mother would only have a silver Christmas tree. There was nothing festive or child-like at this time.

While my brother was in Vietnam, he sent home cassette tapes instead of letters. My Dad gave Arthur the cassette recorder and cassettes before he left. I guess he figured Arthur wouldn't write. My mother would sit in the basement, with the lights out, smoking her five packs of cigarettes, listening to the tapes over and over again. I remember sitting at the top of the basement stairs, mostly listening to Mommy cry. You could even hear gun fire in the background of his tapes. He was in Danang, which was on the front line, and he was a Marine. He was in it! It was an intense time for our family.

During this time, my father had a heart attack, and my brother got to come home from the War. He wasn't home for long while my father was in the hospital. After, he returned from Vietnam my brother and his wife ended up getting stationed in Florida. When Arthur came home for good, most of his friends didn't, but I was a very happy little sister.

Even way back then I was the kid who had a pool and invited all my friends to swim and snack. My Mom used to say, "Ninime," (that's what she called me. I really should find out what that means.) "...you don't want belly friends." I never really got that then. Now I know what she meant. She didn't want me to have friends just for the snacks and the pool. Over the years I brought the phrase "Belly Friend" to a whole new level, so fly on.

Around this time I remember there was a father/daughter dinner at my school that Daddy and I went to. The next day one of the kids asked me why my Dad was so old. I guess I had never really thought of this before. I came home from school and asked my Mom. She said, "We were always going to explain this to you. We adopted you because we wanted a little girl." I remember asking what adoption meant. My Mom, in her perfect way, told me that when people have babies they have to take what they get. When they adopt a baby they pick one out special. As you can imagine, this is the short version of this conversation. When I went to school the next day I told everybody that my Dad was old because I was picked special. My Dad never talked about this with me. I tried, but he wouldn't.

In the next few years, my brother and his wife came home and got a house not too far from us.

Back to nine years old, I was in the bathroom, wiping myself and there was blood. My mother and father were at the Drive-In. My brother was with me and I remember screaming for him. He told me, "Don't worry. Don't be scared, I'm calling Mom." So he gave me the phone and when I said hello, my mother was crying and saying "My baby, my baby, you're too young". My mother never cried, so I got a little nervous. They used to close the concession stand after intermission, so they would get home between 11:00 and 12:00 at night. When she got home, she explained to me about my menstrual cycle. Because my mother was 55 at the time, we had no equipment for this situation. When I was that age, we had to wear garter belts and pads. So, having my period at 9, I developed young.

I am eleven when my brother and his wife had a baby boy. I love that baby more than anything! I baby-sat a lot, and they came to our house every Sunday for dinner. My brother and his wife ended up having another son, so I'm an aunt again! My life was changing dramatically. My brother had a friend who would come to the house when I was babysitting. We'd "fool around" not thinking of it as wrong. He told me, "That's what everybody does." He taught me a lot way too young.

In 2nd grade, there was a rumor around the neighborhood that a family was moving to our quiet neighborhood from the projects of Hartford. The boys in the neighborhood all talked about what it was going to be like. The girls were worried about what they were going to look like. My thoughts were just about the excitement of having more kids around. The oldest of the three boys that moved into the neighborhood was in my class. He was an attention-getting kid named Douglas. In this day and age, he would definitely have been diagnosed with ADHD. He was friends with everybody, some 'cuz they were afraid of him and some 'cuz he was funny. I remember going home from school the first few days he was there, telling my Mom that I liked him.

Time went on, and now we're in 4th grade. We were out on the playground and he asked me if I wanted to walk to the new 7/11. So, we started to walk. Somebody started yelling to me that my Mom was at the school to pick me up for a doctor's appointment. I had forgotten. So, I got in the car and my mother told me, "Stay away from that boy". I told her, "Mommy, I think I'm going to marry him someday." I believe I loved him the first time I saw him.

When we got to 5th grade, Douglas already liked another girl who I was good friends with, but I still liked him. And when you're that young and "going out" with someone, it means you see each other in school and talk on the phone. So, I was "going out" with another boy, and he was "going out" with my friend.

17

So, angels, from my first memories, I mean it when I say: "Life is a Trip". The road is sometimes rough, but it's the rough roads that teach you to balance your attitude of life. It's all about how you handle your roads. Angels,if all the roads were smooth, how would you know your character? Whether you're brave or faithful, strong or weak? Angels, the rough roads I've had are the lessons I've never forgotten. Some of us need to be taught the hard way. Writing this to you angels, I pray your wings fly strong.

Angels, never, ever give up... just let go 'cuz it lightens your flight

ROBBED

It was a Saturday night and in those days my father used to take the deposits from the Drive-In home with us. My mother and father were in the front seat of the car coming home from the Drive-In while I was in the back seat. We drove into the drive way of our dead end street. There were no street lights on our street, so it was very dark.

As my father got out of the car, two guys in ski masks came from the back of our house. They both had large guns. I was getting out of the car right after my Dad. So my door was already open. One of them pulled me out of the car. They told me to lie on my stomach and held a gun to my head. My mother had come out of the hospital one month before this from a heart attack. She never moved from the car and they never told her to.

They told my father to give them all the money he had. My father tried to talk to them. They just screamed about the money, so, he gave them the deposit and the cash in his wallet and they told us not to move until we couldn't

19

see them anymore. They walked backwards
down our dead end street. Backwards down
the brook, and up the path to the golf course
that was next to our house. Daddy got me up
off the ground. He helped my mother out of the
car, went into the house and called the police.

DO SI DO

Looking back on 7th grade, I really acted much older than I was. I babysat for my nephews a lot, and my parents treated like I was older. I made money working at the Drive-In, fixing speakers, popping corn, cleaning and such. I was a good daughter cleaning and helping with house stuff, a good aunt and a great student.

Okay, so I'm in 7th grade and my friend asked me if I wanted to join square dancing with her. We'd been talking about it for a while because my brother and his wife had moved into an apartment and the family that owned the house square danced. Their girls were a little older than me, always cool, and of course there was a boy too!

When I told my Mom I was going to join a square dancing club, she loved the idea. I went to the first meeting or lesson with my friend. That's where I met Birdie. The girls upstairs from my brother were very involved. My good friend Barb knew Birdie too but was not really into square dancing. My best friend

Jody wasn't into it at all, but I loved it and I was a pretty good square dancer!

Now Birdie's whole family was involved in running lessons, bringing us to jamborees, and dances all over. Looking back at it all it seems like a whole other life. I remember my Mom taking me to get my square dancing petticoats, skirts, blouse and shoes. Since I was never really this interested or excited about anything before, she was very happy.

Suzie, one of the girls that lived in the apartment over my brother always helped me get ready. She showed me how to tie "tight" elastic around my petticoat and skirt to make it shorter and very shapely. Birdie's Mom never approved of the way we wore our outfits, but I thought it was so cool that I looked like the older girls.

Suzie had a younger brother who was older than me and we kind of liked each other. On the way home from square dancing one night it was me and Suzie's brother in the back seat. On that ride I had my first kiss. To make a very long story shorter, Suzie's brother and I kissed a few times, held hands, and danced together, but that's about it. I liked this boy a lot, but I really liked another boy more.

Adopting me in their middle age years made my parents seem older than other parents. So, like grandparents (which is what they were) they trusted me and spoiled me. Also, by this time, my Mom had had two heart attacks and was getting sicker. My Dad owned an eyeglass business and ran the Drive-In, which was open 7 nights a week.

Around the time I was 12, the boy I liked a lot, finally asked me out. We'd go to dances, make out and he'd come over to the pool at my brother's apartment. And I could walk through the golf course at the back of my house to meet him halfway from his house. We were together a lot that year.

I got strep throat for the 100th time that year and the doctor said I had to have my tonsils out. My boyfriend came to see me in the pediatric part of the hospital 'cuz I was only 12. When he came I couldn't talk, I could only write. How embarrassed I was, but he just laughed. When I came home he was there with ice cream and we sat holding hands, etc. in my room. He was 16 and in three months I would be 13.

Being adopted you always have weird thoughts about who your parents could be. My neighbor Judy was adopted and we used to pretend we had the same Mom or Dad. We'd say "Ya never know!"

You know how you wonder sometimes what event happened to change your life? Well here's mine, angels. I found a picture in my house, and went to the bathroom to hold it up to my face. She looked a lot like me. After staring at this picture for a long time, I took it to my Mom and asked her who it was. At this point in my life, my angel was always my Mom. I could ask her stuff and she'd tell me. My friends would talk to her 'cuz they couldn't talk to their own Moms like that. I remember my Mom calling my Dad and as I look back, I'm sure she told him not to come home.

My Mom told me the picture was Patricia, Daddy's other daughter we used to visit who had 3 kids. I asked her, "If I'm adopted Mom, how can I look so much like Daddy's daughter?" She answered, "Well honey, we were going to tell you when you were older, but here it goes." So, my Mommy angel told me, through cigarette smoke and a few tears, that Pat was my birth mother. She had come for a visit to my parents in the trailer park. She had gone out and never came back for me. My Mom said I had a big belly like the starving kids and that when Pat never came back they adopted me.

I can't put into words what that day felt like. I had only heard horrible things about Pat all my life. I finally understand why my Dad would get really mad at me and yell "PATRICIA"! I told my Mom I was going to Judy's house, and that I would be home tomorrow. My mother had told me not to forget I just had my tonsils out, so I should rest at Jody's. I called the boy and I went out the front door.

He met me at our spot. "What happened?" was all he could say and I burst out crying. To get the full extent of the feeling of this day, angels, I tried to live up to the stories I had heard of Pat, so I had sex for the first time. This boy and I had done other things, some of it I had learned from my brother's friend, some this boy had taught me. He used to say, "That's how you show you love me". That day I wanted to run away with him and get married. I went home and called Jody. She came over and we talked all night. I turned 13 without my tonsils or my virginity.

I started 8th grade very uh....popular I guess. The boy and I were still very close. He had his driver's license and my parents trusted me. We were together a lot. I believed we would be together forever.

It was after Thanksgiving when we knew we had to talk to our parents. I had missed two periods and I had to come up with a story. So, I told my Mom a very elaborate story that I had been raped. I cried a lot which was easy 'cuz I was a very scared little girl. Assuming that my Mom believed me I carried on and on and on. After I don't know how long my Mom took my tear-filled face in her hands and said, "Now tell me the truth". I had a time of it, trying to convince her I was telling the truth but in the face of the patience of my Mommy angel, I let the truth out. At the end of my confession, my Mom said, "I have to call your brother." Because the boy also told his parents they called for a meeting.

We really thought getting married and having a baby would be the perfect life. At 13 and 16, I guess that would have been a book in itself angels. WOW.

So the meeting included my parents, his parents and us, on his front porch. His father had done a lot of work at the Drive-In for my Dad and neither of them wanted to be at this meeting. I could feel that even at 13. So the confident vocal Moms were debating what to do about this situation. When his mother decided that they would take the baby and raise it, my Dad got really antsy to say the least. He actually got up and said "I will wait in the car". The Mom's told me and the boy to go in the house.

Soon his Mom came in and told us everything was settled. I guess I thought they would tell us the decision but when I walked outside, my Mom said, "Get in the car". We drove the five minutes home, which seemed like forever. Without a word my Mom and I went into the house. My Dad drove away. She began to explain to me all of the reasons I should not have a baby. She explained the reason she called my brother. She told me he knew someone who could help "take care" of this situation. Now, remember, it's a very different time. This was all happening somewhere around the time when Jeannie on the old TV show "I Dream of Jeanie" wasn't even allowed to show her belly button. The world was not as free and open as it is now. We didn't learn about things as young as kids do now.

So the boy and I are still together, planning, dreaming 'cuz we didn't have to worry about getting pregnant. I had told my best friends Jody and Birdie and he was bragging too. Time passed, and one night my Mom said, "You are going to be taking Thursday and Friday off from school." I asked why and she said, "We have to go to New York to take care of your situation." Not understanding, I asked her again, "Why?" At that point my Mom told me that abortion was illegal in Connecticut, but my brother knew a place in New York that could "take care of it".

So, Arthur came over in the morning and my Mom and I went with him to New York City. We went down a long hallway to a room on the left. As we walked in my Mom told me,

"Don't worry honey it will all be over soon."
This is so difficult to think about 'cuz of the way
I feel about life now, but I had no idea what I
was doing then.

The lady told me and my Mom that it
was much better this way and that it was
wonderful that I was so early in my pregnancy.
I think it was then I asked my Mom, "Are they
going to kill my baby or give it to someone
else?" I remember my Mom was now in tears,
which didn't happen often. She told me, "No,
honey, the baby isn't alive yet". I believed that.
That was the first of many things I brought to
my Savior, but, this was the most severe.

They called my name. I had to go in
another room alone. My brother wished me
good luck, my Mom gave me a hug and I went. I
could hear and feel every Moment, every turn
of the tool the man was holding inside of me. I
changed that day.

The lady came and helped me get
dressed. "The procedure went well." she said.
And then she brought my Mom in to see me.
She asked us to sit down and at she started to
explain to me how to take my new birth control

pills...at 13. That's right. Angels, I clearly remember looking at my mother in what I'll call now, horror. I remember her telling me, "You'll never stop having sex now".

So the ride home was quiet, to say the least. My Mom and brother talked. I sat in the back knowing my baby was gone...just gone.

That was the beginning of my downward spiral. It took years for me to understand this was really all connected to me knowing who my birth mother was.

Psalm 34:18 "The Lord is near to them who are of a broken heart."

So many memories rush into my head while writing. Angels, I'm trying not to weigh

down my journey. Let me just say….Life is a Trip….Fly on.

HIGH SCHOOL BUZZ

High School, here we go. First of all let me say, being on birth control at 13… *really* not a good idea.

The summer before high school started, I had lost my boyfriend who I had thought was going to be with me forever. I lost friends over it because they chose sides. I'd walk to our spot often and just sit and write poetry. One of the girls slipped and told me he had a new girlfriend younger than me. So, I bought some paint and Jody and I painted her driveway with not nice stuff.

One day, sitting on the wall at our spot, this car came by. I knew all the boys in the car. They said, "Come on, we'll go for ride" and they had alcohol. Back then the legal age was 18 to drink and two of them were. So we're driving, drinking, laughing, and they stop. They took a bottle, pouring the alcohol all over my face, with me trying to keep my mouth shut. There were 6 boys, one of them held my mouth open, one held my arms and the others touching. My pants came down and they did nasty, horrible things to me in that ride the summer before high school. These boys even knew all that had already happened to me.

They dropped me back off at the wall where my notebook was waiting. Crying in disgust of myself for even getting in that car, I sat on the golf course in between my house and my old boyfriend's. I cried, sore and feeling nasty. Until writing this book, I have never told anyone. I blamed myself, I trusted them, I knew them. It was bad enough everyone knew what had already happened, then to add this nastiness to it...So looking back angels, this event also changed me.

This summer Jody and I worked at the Drive-In a lot. Two boys would come up in the afternoon while we worked on speaker junction boxes. We'd have music just blaring in the projection booth through all the speakers in the lot of the Drive-In. We'd swing on the swings at the playground, and talk. I told them to come back on the weekend for the movies and I'd get them in for free. We had a few make out sessions with them.

This was also the summer I started shop-lifting. The first time I ever got caught I was 14 at "Two Guys" on the Berlin turnpike, right near the Hartford Drive-In. They called my father, and he came. The guy shook his hand and I realized they knew each other from the Chamber of Commerce they were both on. I swore a lot then, so I can't write what I was thinking, but you can imagine. I had already given back all the stupid stuff I had in my pockets, so my Dad looked at me with the middle vein popping out of his head and said, "What do you say young lady?" So I said, "I'm sorry, I won't do it again." We walked outside and my Dad said, "Put your bike in the car". We started to drive toward the Drive-In and he said, "If you want or need something, ask me." And that was it, like it never happened.

So did I stop? I just got better and better at it. They didn't have the stuff to catch shoplifters like they have now. So all through high school I lifted things; things for me and things for my friends.

Before high school started I told my Mom that I wanted to go to Goodwin Tech for hairdressing. She said, "Absolutely not; too many bad boys and drugs there." Well, I guess that wasn't the only place they were. And bad girls, well, we were everywhere! I didn't want to go to our town high school because I felt all the kids knew what had happened.

Ninth grade was horrible except for boys. I guess I was trying to kill the pain in my heart. Working at the Drive-In on the weekends my buddy June, had a brother who started working there too. He asked me out. Of course he was a bit older than me, but my Dad loved June so everything was okay. I was still on birth control and acting much older than I was, so I thought this relationship was for forever too. I don't have any bad memories of him, but I don't want to get too graphic. Then there was Brian from school. He was a pot head who I smoked my first joint with. He was the only boyfriend I never had sex with, but only 'cuz he was like a buddy, I guess. His parents let him drink a lot. Then there was another boy who I met working at the Drive-In too. I liked him a lot, a few boys in between, but in the back of my head was always The Boy, Douglas.

I had a lot of parties downstairs in my rec room, which was where the bar was when my parents used to have parties there. Now, it was more. It had a pool table and a pool in the back. My Mom was getting weaker so she never came down and my Dad wasn't home much. Barb, Jody, and I heard you could get totally high eating aspirin and drinking Coke. Well, we ate and drank a lot...nothing. There are lots more stories like this, but let's fly on through high school.

Now I tell my Dad I want to buy a car. I've been driving my Mom's Impala, but I make enough money for my own car payments. Daddy paid my car insurance out of the ten dollars a week I paid toward the household expenses. He had been teaching me to drive since I was 14 so, 'cuz I am now only known as "Buzz" pretty much, I asked my Dad if I could have a plate that said that on my own car when I got one. More on that later.

So, on through 10th grade I go.

I used to go to Mrs Gieger's house and watch her do hair. That's really what I wanted to do, be a hairdresser and work at home to be with the 12 kids I wanted. All the other Moms were out working except for my poor Mom, who was getting weaker. Now she only sat on the couch and smoked. She was in and out of the hospital with heart attacks.

I looked forward to getting my driver's license, even though I was already driving. I became the taxi during school. But, by May of 10th grade I had basically stopped going to school. I forged notes, which was easy 'cuz Mom was always sick and she didn't get the mail. I only went to my two favorite teacher's classes, English and History, sometimes Math but never ever Gym.

Now, you must understand, Douglas was "Mr High School". He did football, classes, plays, dances, swim team diver; everything I

Sadie Hawk... ...Hot

was not. The boy from the Drive-In was more like me at the time and we got really close. By the end of 10th grade, there was a Sadie Hawkins dance, where a girl has to ask the boy. I asked this boy if he minded me asking Douglas because the boy was supposed to be from Newington High and my boyfriend wasn't. He said okay, 'cuz, I guess, he trusted me, so Douglas and I went together. My Dad was not happy. That summer I became Douglas' "first", in my parent's basement no less. Oh my.

As the memories come, some good, some bad, there are many other stories within these, too many really! And me, still looking for love in all the wrong places and trying to dull pain I didn't even know I had, but...it was fun for that flying lesson, nobody died yet. Fly on...

My Dad took me to get a brand new car. For some reason I fell in love with a florescent orange Datsun B-210. My Dad came back from talking with the guy and told me they only had a standard transmission. I didn't care. I wanted it, so I got it. For about a week Daddy taught me at the Hartford Drive-In how to stop on the big hill and start up, stop and start up. If you've never driven or been taught to drive a standard you can't imagine my Daddy's vein in the middle of his forehead. But, after one week, I was really good. I made my first car payment and in about one month my MEBUZZ plates came. Quite the conversation starter on the road!

So Birdie, Jody and I decide to go to Hampton beach for a week. That week was high and higher! My Dad knew somebody who had a camper there, and we had a blast. And, like before, so many stories within this story!

So on we fly through High school.

By 11th grade, I was only attending two classes, English and Art. This is the year I started hanging with a guy I had known for a long time. He and I always had weed and money, and I had the car. We were a perfect pair. He was another boy I never had sex with. I think, looking back, that was only 'cuz we were always too wasted.

In 11th grade, a "friend with many benefits" became a security guard at a store in Hartford. We actually fooled around a lot, a *lot*.

Benefits knew that I was a shoplifter, so he came up with a scheme. I'd bring him to work, take some clothes, while he, the security guard, would turn his head. Then I'd bring the clothes back to the store and get the cash for them. I can't remember the split, but it wasn't 50/50; it was more like 20/80, Benefits with the 80. That went on until he, I can't remember why, stopped working there. He made a lot of money.

Oh wait, I forgot my first accident. In the car was, me, Birdie, Marylou and Mac and two more I can't remember. We were stopped with the blinker on, to go left into 7/11. In the rearview mirror I saw a car coming directly at us. I grabbed the steering wheel and I braced

on the clutch and the brake. Wham! We got pushed. Marylou got out and went to the other car. She screamed at the driver, "Where'd you get your license; in an F***ing Cracker Jack box?" We're in the middle of the road and a cop comes. Remember angels, there were no cell phones then. None of us were really hurt 'cuz we were all so high it didn't matter. Of course, the cop knew my father. So when he came up to me he said, "I will call your Dad". The car was not drivable so it got towed. In three days I had it back because Daddy fixed it, like the accident had never happened.

One day my weed buddy asked if I'd pick his brother up in Hartford who was getting out of jail that day. Of course, I said yes. I can't remember who came with us, but I waited in the car and out they came. And of course, his brother sat in the front with his gorgeous blue eyes and we talked. He was very happy to be out. I was still steady with the boy from the Drive-In when those bad boy brothers asked me to a party. Of course, I said yes. So, I called my boyfriend and told him I was giving them a ride to a party and I might stay a while. He said, "Ok".

So, we're at this party, drinking and getting high and I'm with the out-of-jail brother. Sometime in the night he asked me if I was drinking the punch and I asked why. He told me the punch was laced with LSD. He was protecting me I guess, but I was drinking beer, so it was all good. Back then, acid, pot, and speed were okay; LSD was *scary*.

Later that week I was at the brothers' house, skipping school and partying. I will never forget what happened. This kid came over and I stayed in the living room while they were in the kitchen. This kid got beat bad, 'cuz he didn't have the money he owed them. My buddy looked at me and said, "Let's go Buzz". I still think about that poor kid. The out-of-jail brother went back to jail soon after that. We had a few good Moments though. He was an angel of protection one night without even knowing it. You just never know who or what the Lord will use to speak to you. So angels, try to listen.

Flying through high school; so many stories to tell, not enough paper in the world.

In this time somewhere the Junior Prom came and I guess I assumed I would go with Douglas. I bought the dress, but he took someone else.

For my second car accident, I was taking a left when I slipped on ice hit a huge truck. My car, of course, was totaled. I lose track of accidents about five accidents later with this same poor orange Datsun B-210, which I had named Petunia.

One time, my old boyfriend Brian was in my driveway, his car was parked in front of mine and I was having a party at my house. My parents went away for the night and we were all very drunk so Brian was mad 'cuz he didn't realize that Douglas was coming to this party. Brian got in his car and punched it. We heard a terrible crash. He had backed up and smashed my car. He totaled it. That time, even Daddy couldn't fix it; she was dead!

So, we went looking and I bought a Datsun 610-510-something-10. Even though it was blue it was standard so it resembled my orange Datsun.

I had quit high school on my 18th birthday. I'd had enough; I wanted to do hair. Senior prom comes. Again, for Senior Prom I assumed I would go with Douglas, but he asked someone else. By this time my Mom and Dad

43

could not stand Douglas 'cuz he caused me too many tears. Later Douglas tells me, "I didn't want to take you and just leave you there and go do my thing." (After being married to "Mr High School" for 30 years, I understand that now, but at the time it just hurt.) So instead of going with Douglas, like I had assumed, I parked at the Drive-In with June and Birdie and others on Senior Prom night. Birdie was a year behind me in school so it wasn't her prom that night. Barb went with Birdie's brother.

I think, if I'm not confused on the timing, I was going out with June's brother. He was a bit older than me, worked at the Drive-In, and was cute. We spent lots of time together and I loved his family. My Dad and Mom liked him; he was fun.

During these days somewhere, enters Brian Neville. He was the roadie for a band and Douglas worked with him. I'd go with them sometimes since the band and roadies could drink at the bars for free. I got to know lots of bartenders and Neville, who was a really cool, nice guy.

I will end high school with this. Fly on.

The next event was graduation. Mutual friends told me that Douglas had gotten a Football scholarship to Tennessee Tech. I was trying to be happy for him. I went to his graduation to see him and all my friends graduate. Of course, that night we got together and he told me about his scholarship. He said he was nervous because he knew everybody in our town and everybody knew him, so he would be starting a new life. A few days later he came to my house with a rose. I walked outside to the driveway and he handed me the rose. I started to get teary 'cuz he was leaving for four years. Then he said, "Look closer". On the rose was a pearl ring he wanted me to wear and wait for him. My parents weren't happy about this but I was.

So, people come and go in your life angels. Some you choose to forget, some you'll remember even when you don't want to. In my trip of life I have learned the ones you truly love you never forget. Somewhere inside you they are burned in. Love comes with pain, loneliness, disappointment, heartache, and lots of work. True love is worth the work. In this valley of my travel, I had a pearl ring that made it worth it to me.

So angels keep your head straight, your hopes high, and fly on.

DOUBLE Ds

(Drinkin' and Druggin')

This was the year when I was introduced to black beauties aka speed. I had taken some beauties, bought some paint, and was coming home going 95 on Maple Hill Avenue when I got pulled over. The speed limit was only 35. The cop took my license and said, "You're Dick Buzzell's daughter." He told me to follow him to my house. He said, "Stay in the car." He went to the door and rang the bell. He and my Dad laughed and talked and looked at me. The cop walked by my car to get to his and said, "Your father will take care of you." I'm thinking, "Oh good, good" 'cuz Daddy won't do anything. My Dad waves for me to come in. He hands me my license and says, "Not so fast, be careful." That's it.

So I went back outside fast because I was speeding and got my paint. My Dad left for work and I started to paint the entire Rec room bright yellow with black trim. I painted Mickey Mouse on a wall, who knows why. In the pool table room were movie posters and such so that room was already cool.

The next morning, after I have been up all night, my Mom asked, "What did you paint?" So I told her, probably really fast, that I had painted the whole rec room. I had wanted to finish it so I had to stay up all night. Then I got dressed and went to hair dressing school.

When I started hairdressing school I was the happiest I thought I could get. My Dad was also very happy; I'd always have work, being that work was his thing. My instructors were the best really, even though I didn't appreciate them at the time. Miss Elmo was very old and wise, Miss Deb was very strict, and Miss Bruna was the exotic, creative one. I loved them all, but not everybody did. I had no favorite of the three 'cuz they were so very different from each other. I learned a lot from each one. Tracy, Richard, and Melanie were my best buddies in hairdressing school. The girl with the beauties was one of my favorites and I can't even remember her name. I guess my brain doesn't think that's important 'cuz I have tried.

The public came into the school for hair care and that was "the floor". We were supposed to be in school for eight weeks before you were put on the floor. I had been in school four weeks when Miss Elmo asked if I thought I was ready to take the floor. The school happened to be very busy that day and I said, "Oh yeah!" She asked me if I was nervous, I said no. She said, "I'm here if you need me."

My first customer was a wash and set with lots of teasing. When I had finished, the lady was very happy and I had my first regular customer every week. Miss Elmo told me that day that I was a natural. Angels, that was the best thing an instructor could have ever said to me. Miss Elmo, being the oldest, wisest, and having the longest career of hairdressing became my hair Angel. Of course, I was on cloud nine, always being high anyway.

I still worked at the Drive-In and partied a lot. Birdie was working for her brother at a very busy cafeteria. They needed help with cooking, serving, cleaning, etc, so Birdie was my boss. This is where I met Patty. We all got high, drugged, drank a lot.

One night we were working hard and, as usual being the end of the night, we were doing dishes, mopping, and whatever else needed to be done. Patty kind-of collapsed. Thinking back, Birdie and I probably did very well. This is how we found out Patty was an epileptic and didn't always take her medication right. Birdie, Patty and I got really close and still partied a lot together.

After I got my cosmetology license the school called me and said I've been offered a job. It was in West Hartford at a salon in Bishops corner called "Cut and Curl". It was a prestigious part of town. I went for my interview, and I was hired.

So, I'm working in a salon with nine other operators. It was a *little* competitive. The nine of us got along very well and all partied together. Me, Val, Lisa, Venus, and Juan were probably the closest. Lisa was lots of laughs...lots of everything. Juan brought me to my first gay bar ad my first mushrooms. Val was my buddy, my pal. Venus and I, we would have vodka in our soda cans and lines of coke in the bathroom waiting for each other. Back then smoking was not banned so there was lots of that too. All of us were big money-makers.

Mrs Barret owned the salon but was not a hairdresser. Then, came the sale of the salon, to Miss Concetta, who *was* a hairdresser. She had bought the business about three years after I started. She taught me a lot about hair and people. I became very important to her 'cuz I made a lot of money.

Once, she caught me coming out of the bathroom with white powder on my nose. She asked because she really didn't know. So I explained. In the words of Connie, "Please be careful." Not, "You're fired", just, "Be careful." Does this sound like my Dad? Her reason was the business I brought in for her.

Douglas was still at Tennessee Tech and every time I talked to him I just wanted him home. I still have every letter he wrote to me from Tennessee. He's not a writer so I cherish them.

There were other boys during this time. Brian was trying very hard with me and I knew Douglas was having a good time there, 'cuz that's what he did. So I wrote and told him I thought I was pregnant 'cuz I had missed a period. He called and we talked for a long time about it. He came home, nineteen hours on a bus. I was overjoyed. Brian was not. Neither was Douglas's father. He brought him all the way back to Tennessee.

I don't know how long but soon after this Douglas got heat stroke while playing football on astroturf. Again he came home nineteen hours on the bus. This is when we started talking seriously about getting married.

When Douglas came to ask for my hand in marriage my Dad said, "Over my dead body." Douglas said, "Whatever it takes Mr. B." My mother and father had watched me cry so many times over him. When I asked my mother for the diamond my Dad's Mom left me, she was a bit nervous. She told me that she knew I loved him and I would do it anyway. Douglas and I become engaged, set our wedding date for October 6, 1979.

Fly on...

Before we were married, Douglas and I went out riding one night with all our biker buddies. We ended up at a bar by the beach and I was sitting at a table with the only other girl riding with us. We were watching a girl at the bar pinching Douglas every time she walked by us. So I guess I finally had enough, and being the non-fighter that I am, I stuck my hand out. I said, "Could you leave him alone. We're engaged." She grabbed my hand and bent it backwards breaking my knuckles. I went back to my table and crazy Sue gave me a bottle and told me to break it over her head. So being only 5'2" and the girl looked about 6 feet, I tippy toed to reach her with the bottle over her head and she turned around. Then she beat the crap out of me. I had a tube top on which came off and on. The guys we rode with are gathered in a circle screaming for me to punch. All I can think is, "Douglas where are you?" Then, she gets pulled off me by her hair. My larger than life angel saved me. He was back.

Getting up off the floor, putting my shirt back on, I watched this girl try to beat the crap out of a man with the nickname "Animal". So, Douglas when finally got control of it, we went back to the hotel where Douglas lived.

The next morning my hand was huge, so we had to go to the hospital. My parents, of course, thought he broke my hand 'cuz they didn't believe my story. I was in a cast for a while. Not good when you're a hairdresser. Not one of my better memories.

The saying goes, "You only hurt the ones you love". And Douglas has hurt me 'til I feel I can't go on. He saved me a few times; I know he loves me. I think we hurt the ones we love, kid to parent, sister to sister, friend to friend, husband to wife, because we are secure they will always love us. I've done pretty well in this area, I think. I've tried to never hurt anyone. And the ones who have hurt me, I try to love them. I was hanging with lots of people at that time who were injuring my wings. Love makes my baggage lighter to travel with.

"There are two ways to fly through life...one as if *nothing* is a miracle...the

other as if *everything* is a
miracle."-Albert Einstein

"JUST THE WAY YOU ARE"

Dad had told me on the morning of my wedding, "He drinks too much. It will be a very hard life for you, but he's Polish so he'll always

work." My Dad; gotta' love him. Walking me down the aisle my Dad kept saying, "We can leave, you don't have to do this."

By this time my Mom had become so weak that

she couldn't walk downstairs to the hall for the reception. Douglas and Arthur made a chair with their arms and brought her down. She looked up the stairs at me, smiled and winked. It was like she was saying, "He's okay". My Mom had always told me if she lived to see me get married she'd be happy. Six months later she died. This event took some wind from my wings.

Clouded with alcohol and drugs my favorite memory of the wedding is when we had to get my girls in from the parking lot getting high to catch the bouquet.

I had picked a song by Billy Joel called "Just the Way You Are" for our wedding. My larger-than-life angel has tested that over the years, but this year he fired it up. Although the hole in my heart is healing, I still believe that song.

I had thought up until this year that I had gone through my hottest fires; I was wrong. I have a favorite quote that always speaks my heart:

"I know God doesn't give me more than I can handle. I just wish He didn't trust me so much."-Mother Theresa

Before we got married we bought a tiny yellow house in Bristol, CT. It needed a lot of work. Douglas was working at Pratt and Whitney and I was at Cut and Curl. We were both making very good money but also spending. People in my life who remember that house just laugh. It was so small but the parties there were huge. This is the house where we welcomed our new baby. As I look back it was like another life, but I wouldn't change a thing. These things are what make me who I am.

In our very dysfunctional little neighborhood there were four couples we became close with. Four very different couples were all dysfunctional in their own unique way;

a well-off couple from family money, a state cop and his family, a blue collar comedy couple, and an entrepreneur and his wife. All four of these couples are now divorced. Being very drunk all the time kind-of clouds how very wrong things were. Douglas was close to each of the guys, I was not close to the wives. I don't know how we made it through all this, other than by the grace of God.

In the first year we were married I went out one night with Birdie to Fantasy Factory to go dancing and drinking. Fantasy Factory was a bar that had a huge impact on these days. This is the place that the girls in my wedding and I went the night before my wedding. Birdie and I went to a party at a guy's house after. Birdie got in a problem with a girl and ended up with a black eye. It was the first time I didn't come home all night and Douglas went to my Daddy's house looking for me. So, I get home and life goes on.

Fly on...

MY FOUR ANGEL BABIES, ETC...

Matthew, Leah, DJ, Kimberly

I'm 24, married four years and I'm going to have a baby. The baby I have wanted forever is coming. These are very active alcohol and drug abuse days, which, to me, was normal. I remember when I told Connie I was pregnant she was kind of mad. I really thought she was going to cry. "You can't do that to me." she said. I was one of her busiest money-making operators, hairdressing was my life.

My first angel baby was extremely active in my belly, especially when I was dancing or partying. I can remember being at a party once and one of the guys there rubbed my belly and said I would be an awesome Mom. I had already lost my Mom but my Dad was excited and my larger-than-life angel, Douglas, was out of his mind.

Before I had my first baby I was going to work one day, where my belly was getting so big I could barely reach my customer's heads. I had stopped at Lynn's to buy some weed on my way to work. We got high, then I left to get into my car and my water broke. Boy, oh boy did I have water! I went into a package store to call Douglas and tell him. There was a kid working at this package store behind the counter who looked about 18. Looking back I remember his face watching a women soaking wet with a huge belly walking towards him. I was high and the first thing I did in that package store was get buy pint of vodka and asked if he had a phone I could use. He said to me, "Do you want me to call the hospital?" He gave me the phone and I called Douglas who said, "Oh no, no, no, not today." It was a Saturday and he was working on his car.

61

So my first gift from heaven that I didn't deserve arrived February 3, 1983. Douglas came back to the hospital about 4 am very drunk and crawled in bed with me. My roommate could not take this much excitement and pushed her button. Needless to say the nurse asked him to leave. After a little begging from us he left. Before he left he kind of boasted, "You had the most beautiful baby in the hospital Poop!" I'm sure I answered, "I know." (Poop is what Douglas has called me 'cuz I never liked the way he says "Gwen")

We had juggled a few names around, one of which was Harley David...Get it?! But when he was born we looked at each other, and Douglas Joseph Jr. came to be. You will get to know him better through my journey.

My brother-in-law Eddie came to visit at the hospital and brought me nip bottles. To me Eddie was my hero that day. My step mother-in-law Viola had thrown me a huge baby shower, Birdie and Jody threw one, my boss and hairdressers I worked with too. I was very blessed by all these angels and so was my perfect little DJ.

After DJ was born I started working closer to home in Connie's other salon in Bristol. The girls in Bristol also became fellow flyers. They were Karen, Betsy and Darlene and we all worked well together.

Now I'm twenty five. Douglas came home one day and said, "I found a perfect house for us." We looked, we bought. I loved the house too; it was bigger for more kids and bigger parties. That house has so many memories for us, good, and dark, dark bad.

Now we live in a big, beautiful four bedroom house, perfect for parties and all that accompanies that. One memory of my larger than life angel is when we were having a New Year's Eve party. He bumped his head on my kitchen light for the last time and pulled it out of the ceiling. Somewhere around this time our buddy, who always stayed up with me when Douglas went to bed and everybody else left, told me that if we ever got divorced or Douglas left me, he would always take care of me. I loved him so much, but only like a brother. When Douglas got sober, I told him that for some reason, and that was the end of this friendship. I miss him even after all these years, my stay up forever, caring Angel.

To fly you through this, I thought my life was perfect. DJ was starting to walk, Douglas was still working his good job at Pratt and Whitney and I was working closer to home at Connie's other salon. But Douglas was addicted "full speed ahead" to cocaine. I guess through my own addiction, I didn't realize how bad it was.

One day a guy came to the door one day that I knew to be a bad, bad guy. He had a gun under his blazer and was smoking a joint. I was holding DJ and I let him in. He said "Where's Dougie? He owes me". Douglas was upstairs. I went to tell him and he gave me a wad of money to give the guy. That's when I thought, "Can I raise another baby in this?" I had a drug problem too but living with a larger than life man who had larger than life anger made the situation, as I look back, intense. The visit from the guy made things clearer to me.

I went outside to get the mail and Douglas locked me out of the house. DJ was in the house with his Dad. Douglas was going from door to door making sure I couldn't get in. He was holding the baby and I was crying and begging him to let me in. I think what finally did it since he was so high, was DJ screaming for his Mommy. Douglas finally let me in and life went on.

My half-brother Keith called me. I was so excited 'cuz he wanted to come and get to know me. Douglas was afraid for me, but he knew it was important to me so Keith came to stay with us.

He called for me to pick him up at the bus station. I went and on the way back to my house we tried to get to know each other. He told me that he had gotten clean from drugs and alcohol. But, after a very short time with us, he was back to it. During this visit things went on that I would like to believe I have erased.

Right around that same time Douglas woke me up with a butcher knife running across the spindles of the stairway, yelling irrational things at me! When he was like this I would pretend to be sleeping. He came upstairs, picked up the mattress, and I was on the floor.

Then he cried and apologized and said he would never do it again.

Around this time I realized I was pregnant again so I called my friend Jody. We went to West Hartford and I aborted this baby. After that trip, we went to Lynn's and did everything an addict would do to dull the pain.

A week or so later I came home from work to see the phonebook opened to "Taxi's" and Keith was gone. We had partied with him, fed him, got him a job. We did too much I guess. Douglas flew up the stairs when he got home. He had kept a lot of money in his dresser and it was all gone. My father tried so hard to warn me not to trust any of my blood relatives, no matter how much I wanted to know them. Now, at age 49, I get that lesson. But, we all have to fly for ourselves.

Fly on angels.

I now find out that I am pregnant with my second gift from heaven. Douglas is getting worse. The visit from the guy with the gun is still in my mind. I wanted this baby so, so, so bad and my Douglas did too. I told him I was pregnant again and that he had to get himself together, of course, still believing *I* had no problem. Soon after, he told me he went to his boss at Pratt and Whitney and he was going to get help. Drinking and drugging were still a large part of me. I guess 'cuz I'd gone on so long like this, it was normal.

So at twenty-six my second angel baby was on her way. In the ultrasound she was sucking her thumb. In those days they couldn't know girl or boy, but I was hoping for a girl. We juggled lots of names for her too. I really wanted to name her after my Mom somehow but my Mom had hated her name, Marjorie. So we chose *her* mother's name, Leah.

My Leah arrived on May 10, 1985. You must fly very fast to know my Leah better. My larger than life angel was clean and sober when his baby girl was born.

Somehow, with his new addiction to AA meetings, Douglas wasn't home much. My Douglas was now addicted to buying buildings, making money, or what I think was trying to fill the hole he had inside. We now owned a restaurant, and a six family building in the

 middle of
Hartford,
all while
still
working
at Pratt
and
Whitney.
He had
borrowed
money
from my
Dad, his Dad, and used it to put up our house.
Me, I'm just being a Mom, a hairdresser, a wife,
counselor sometimes to friends, and, yes, an
addict. A functional addict, but an addict
nonetheless.

I thank God today for AA, because
that's how Douglas met John the Cook. I first
met John when Douglas brought him home, as
his sponsor in AA. If you don't know what that
means, here it is. A sponsor is your go-to
person when you need flight help in staying
clean and sober.

John became a very important part of
our family. The first few years he was Douglas'

friend and brother. John helped Douglas heal parts of his terribly broken wings. I was still using so I only knew him as my man's sponsor.

← Ellen's Smile

John was a cook at New Britain Hospital, hence the nickname. He was always astonished that our fridge held lots of beer, not as much food as he thought should be there. So he'd cook and cook. I grew to love him like a sort of Mom. I had been cutting his hair through a curly perm phase and blonde streaks and we'd talk.

On my 30th birthday Douglas was afraid me and my posse would get a little out of control. He rented a limo for all of us girls. Terry was too chicken to fly with us that night...and we were flying high. Douglas made breakfast for Birdie, Jody, Nanc, Ellen and I. Looking around the table I thought to myself, "Do I look like them?" The answer my still quiet voice gave me was, "No, no, *much* worse." That was the last night I drank. Other things took longer.

When my little Leah was eleven months old, I found myself pregnant with my third angel.

While I was pregnant, we were at a party at my buddy Nancy's apartment which was on the third floor. Douglas was what we now know as a "sober drunk". Nancy had made eggnog; lots of "nog" with some egg. I sat next to that bowl helping everybody to some and myself to lots. It was time to leave and Nancy had put a chair at each landing. I took a breather on each chair.

This baby's name was going to be Noel for a girl, 'cuz she was supposed to be born around Christmas. If she was a boy her name would be Ryan because while I was pregnant we went to Cape Cod and Ryan O'Neil was filming a movie so the streets were all shut down. We, of course, lurked outside Ryan and Farah's trailer. Waiting for a glimpse, the bodyguard came out and asked what we planned to do with the pictures we planned to take. Ryan O'Neil finally came out, he put his arm around me, and his other hand on my big belly. He asked me my name. I was a little star-struck; I couldn't remember it. He talked to DJ and Leah a little bit. Douglas took the pictures and he had to go.

On January 1, 1987, my angel Kimberly was born. She wasn't named Noel 'cuz my mother in law once told me that if she'd ever had a girl her name would have been Kimberly and she had three boys.

My pure heart of compassion angel Kimber came on New Year's Day. To get to know my third angel, fly gently as she is my gentle spirit.

At this point we still have the restaurant, Douglas is still a welder at Pratt and Whitney and a landlord of a six family

building that ALWAYS has problems. He was still, somehow staying sober... me, not so much! My larger than life angel asks me to sign papers here and there. I trusted him so I signed where he told me to.

I was at an amusement park called Quassy with Ellen and our kids, when he found us. He took me aside and told me we were going bankrupt and losing our house in foreclosure. The whole process took time. Our house was auctioned off on our anniversary. My Dad was going to come to the auction and buy it for us, but at the beginning of that week he had a heart attack. Angels, this makes you understand what's important and what's not. My Dad was much more important than my house.

Around this time, Douglas met a pastor dining in his restaurant. This pastor, answers every question my Douglas ever wanted answered about the Bible. His grandmother, Bobchi, who he loved deeply, was Catholic. Douglas and his brothers were too. Douglas, being a very curious kid, thought a lot about all the Bible stuff that Bobchi tried to teach him. Now, at twenty nine, he tells me all his questions are answered. I remember that I wanted to go to the Episcopal Church down the street with another family in our neighborhood because I wanted to sing in the choir, so I did. That was the extent of religion for me.

But I begin to watch him slowly change. The best way I can explain it, is Jesus was the only balance I have ever seen in him. Everything else, every day was manic. He had very *high* highs... very *low* lows. He never tried to make me believe but he was changing.

So, I now have a home based salon of my own. I'm in the living room on a Monday reading to my kids. The phone rings. It's a doctor asking for Mrs. Malinowski. He asked me if my husband had shared his story with me. I said, "Excuse me?" I then listened to his psychiatrist explain his situation to me. I melted to the floor. I remember all the kids being on the floor with me. I told him, "Thank you for sharing what my husband couldn't or wouldn't". He told me that "by law" he had to.

I made my first call to Douglas at the restaurant. I told him, "Come home right now or we would all be gone". The next call was to my friend Terry. I told her I needed her to take my kids to her house and if she got there before Douglas, I was coming too. She said, "I'm on my way" and never asked a question. He got there first and in about two minutes Terry came. Terry took my three kids and Douglas and I talked. That's when he told me if he didn't tell me his story the doctor would call. This is when my larger than life angel had a break down and ended up in the hospital.

Ok angels life is a trip hold on for my bumps.

I didn't know it that day but I was pregnant with my fourth angel at that time. The saddest thing about that time for me was that Douglas wasn't home and my kids didn't even know it. He had been so busy working his job, running the restaurant, taking care of the six family house, and don't forget the AA meetings and now, church. He had lost about 80 pounds, was drinking three to four pots of coffee a day. I had three kids and a business to run when I realized I was pregnant. So angels, this may be a bit extreme for you, but for me, this was just life. I did it all with a smile.

I brought my kids to see their Daddy only twice. We fed pigeons outside on a bench and they loved it. Now DJ is four years old, Leah is two, Kimberly is one, and Mommy is pregnant. To make everything ok, I just kept being high. We were eating eggs and Mac and cheese most of the time.

I remember vividly my friend, and coke connection, Diane watching my kids so I could go see Douglas. When I got there he was really mad. He wasted our visit 'cuz he was so mad. We sat together and he was crying 'cuz he wrecked our visit over being mad about something stupid. What he didn't quite understand, was that's what I was used to.

His doctor had asked me, "Do you feel like you're on a rollercoaster?" and I said "WOW! Exactly!" I remembered a time when all of us were driving somewhere. I was pregnant, DJ and Leah were in the back, and Douglas said to me, "It would be quick if I drove off this mountain and we would all be together." That's how out of control he was. Now, I was starting to see him kind of lethargic and I thought, "This is not Douglas". But, they were only trying to regulate his medication. I got him calmed down and told him it was okay.

I went home, got the kids, and Diane had to go to work. She was an exotic dancer at the time, which included lots of cocaine. I took the kids to Terry's house. We had a day with all of our kids and me still pregnant. To stay self-medicated I was drunk, high, and on my way home I got pulled over. The three kids were sleeping in the back of the station wagon. When DJ woke up he was very excited about the cop car.

My registration had lapsed so he impounded the car. Me and the kids had to get into the cruiser and he brought us to the police station. The cop told me I had to call someone to pick us up. For some reason I called home. Because I never lock my house Diane had gotten out of work early and was there. She had a tiny car and we packed in the three kids and pregnant me.

She asked me, after we stopped laughing, if I had my pot. It had been there when I left Terry's house. We got home and I put the kids to bed. I checked my pockets again; it was gone. So we had a few drinks and did a few lines.

I talked to Terry the next day to tell her what happened. She asked me what I did in the police station to lose my pot. The only thing I remember doing was going to the bathroom. So, all I could think was I must have dropped it in the police station bathroom.

So angels, even in my messed up life God was protecting me. Even when you don't know enough to choose right He will protect you. He also knew that I would change for him. I believe he protected me for His glory. He knew that the children I was to bear would serve Him. I've loved them more than life.

Before our family met Jesus we were a bit crazy. As I have tried to teach my children about life my children have taught me what life is all about. Thanks guys!

We give our children genes, God gives them grace. We take care of their bodies, God takes charge of their soul.

XOXO

MIRACLES HAPPEN

At this point in my life I was self -
medicating. Drinking and drugs were quite a
crutch by now. Douglas came out of the
hospital but could not come live at home yet.
John the Cook took care of him at his house...I
LOVE THAT!

My most incredible memory of this
whole time in my life was that I had to bring my
3 children to a Department of Children office to
determine if they were safe. They were taken

in separately, one by one, then all three together. I didn't realize it at the time angels, but my God was watching. He knew what I would become, and what I was for my kids. They were, and are, my life.

One of my rockiest roads on this trip of life was when my doctor wanted me to have a test done because she wanted to be sure if the baby had down syndrome or not. At that visit she told me she was pretty sure the baby had down syndrome and that I should seriously consider abortion. Remember with me angels, I can feel this baby moving. My kids and I were talking to this baby.

The only other visitor Douglas had in the hospital was Pastor Paul. I had met him and his wife when Douglas had brought us to church. In my confusion of this baby I called Pastor, and he came. I explained to him, that the doctor told me that I should seriously consider having the baby aborted because I already had three healthy children and a husband who has serious emotional issues. Pastor Paul listened to me and asked me if I would love this baby less if he had down syndrome. I answered quickly, "Absolutely not.

I love this baby already." We talked for quite a while. The other thing I remember is the pastor saying, "God doesn't make any junk". That stuck with me.

I was going to church now. I was also doing lines in the bathroom of the school where the church met even though I had three kids and was pregnant with the fourth.

At one visit to the doctor, she showed me movies of down syndrome children and really tried to sway me her way. By the grace of God I remembered that God doesn't make any junk. Now, I know you are not to tempt the Lord, no deals but I had just started learning and I prayed, "God, if You're really there, heal my baby and I will serve You forever. If You don't, then I was right, You're not there." I believe now as I look back, that I needed to be radically saved and the Lord knew that I would serve Him. God began to heal my baby.

I had my buddy Ellen with me at a doctor's visit. She was truly an angel for me this day! The doctor said I was dilated 5 centimeters and she asked if I wanted to be induced. "OH yes," I answered. So Ellen took my three and her son to my house. Douglas met me at the hospital and my beautiful boy was born. I remember the doctor gasping. She kept saying, "He's healthy."

It took me two days to name him 'cuz I wanted something powerful. I heard that Matthew meant "a gift from God". That was it...Perfect! His middle name is Paul, because without the Lord placing Pastor Paul in my life I don't know what I would have chosen to do.

So on September 9, 1988 my Matthew was born. As we fly through my trip of life you will glimpse the glory of this peaceful Angel; a true miracle just for me from my best friend, JC.

My favorite memory of John the Cook is when we brought Matthew home. He was there with a huge turkey meal... I cried. That day he was my Mom. My DJ was so excited to have a brother and Leah and Kimberly just to have a baby. I remember vividly this day and our giving thanks feast.

Be realistic angels...expect a miracle

ANGEL TANK

I call him Boo. As I write and remember my fight the Lord scared me with my 4th child so...BOO! My God has an incredible sense of humor, just like my Matthew. The birth of this boy was miraculous.

Matthew is my baby, my youngest and maybe a little spoiled. He wanted to play the drums since he was very young. Hearing him and his brother play now takes my breath away. The musical talent of these four kids of mine is absolutely God-given. But, my baby is incredible.

This is also the young man who asked me when I came home from the hospital after the motorcycle accident, if I remembered squeezing his hand. I felt bad saying no, but there was so much then I couldn't remember. He told me he had been holding my hand, with blood still on my pillow from my head, telling me everything would be ok. He told me I squeezed his hand. He told me that's when he knew I would be ok. I can look horrible and scary and my Boo will always say, "Mommy you look beautiful." ...I LOVE THAT!

I watch my granddaughter Jayla when sees her Bubbi. Her whole face lights up. He loves her so much my gentle giant angel.

My angel of humor can make me pee my pants! This young man makes everyone laugh. Matthew makes videos, paintings and writes songs. Tank is my artist angel that dances to the beat of a different drum. Watching him grow up into his own man is becoming one of the most gracious gifts the Lord has given me. He will be 21 this year and

Best Man in his brother's wedding. I am whole heartedly looking forward to the toast he will give.

Angel Tank, as you can imagine, has always been a big boy except before he was five. He was a bit scrawny and then he grew into a Tank. He got the nickname "Tank" from a football coach he had. The coach that gave him that nickname was the same one, who after a million dedicated practices, told him he couldn't play football. Tank didn't make weight. But, in high school he could always play, even with a broken thumb.

Matthew asked me a while ago to pray because he felt something big was going to happen with the band this past summer so I did. The U.N.I.T.E.D. are playing at a Christian event called Soul Fest this summer. This event could be compared to a drug free, alcohol free, Woodstock-like event. They were invited to go to a conference and set up right next to them was the man who runs Soul Fest. God put that man next to them talking with my oldest son and they are now scheduled to play. This is a huge opportunity for my boys as they fly through their faith. I LOVE THAT!

So many stories of my Boo...His first love, of course, was from Camp Faithful...When **he brought half the football team home to color** their hair maroon for a game...Inventing a game **with Kristopher call**ed the "groin throw" and **somehow puncturing himself in the testicle sack with a branch (I DID NOT LOVE THAT, although I have that stick taped in his baby book)**... Praying and jumping for God to make him fly...Now **trying to lose weight for his health and maturing** enough to really do it (I'm so proud)...And, my **personal favorite, once getting so mad at the other three kids that my Matthew said my** favorite line, "IM RUNNING AWAY AND IM TAKING MOMMY WITH ME!". That's my Boo.

Matthew has much more terrain to travel and I know he'll always try to fly high, **and** choose to do what's right.

Luke 1:37 "For with God, nothing shall be impossible."

Mother Theresa has a quote that is exactly my Matthew:

"Never let anyone come to you without feeling happier and better when they leave you".

I love you Boo!

SEASONS CHANGE

February 6, 2009, my angel Kimberly is going to Maine to take her test to get into nursing school this weekend. She is blessed with a young family to stay with, that we here all consider part of our family. Billy and Cathy were her role models and friends when she was younger and that continues to be the case. Now, they have a daughter who has also became a part of our extended family, the always amazing Grace. We've been overjoyed to learn Little Cathy is expecting another baby. I know this young couple is not perfect, but they have been placed in our lives perfectly by God. Cathy has blessed my girls with so much love, including my Jayla; she is an angel without a doubt.

Let me fly you through one of my very special Christmas memories. Billy and Cathy took me to the grocery store and said "Go, Mrs M, this is your Christmas present." I was incredibly overwhelmed then. Even now I feel uplifted in flight. God has chosen to use these two young people together, who were faithful before he let them know they were chosen for each other. "You reap what you sow" has come to pass for these two because of their faithfulness. As I peacefully, thoughtfully, introduce you to Billy and Cathy it brings me back to my Kimber.

This young woman has never bent on what she thought was right. I believe with all that I am, that this is by the grace of God. However, trusting us to raise her is His absolute infinite grace and power, that's the only explanation there is. She was never as rowdy as DJ and Leah were; God's Mercy on me. If I told Kimber, "Don't touch." she just didn't. She lived upright, always faithful to her Creator.

My Kimber was three years old when she, Leah, Matthew and Kristopher were playing hairdresser while I was doing a haircut. They would ring the doorbell to the big old solid oak front door, and Leah would answer it. This particular time Leah slammed the door, not knowing my Kimberly had her fingers on the door jam. I heard a scream that day and I praise God I never heard it again. We opened the door. Blood was everywhere, and my baby was shaking her hand. I wrapped a bath towel around her arm, brought her to the kitchen, sat her on the counter and fell to my knees. By this time I had been going to church for about two years and that didn't enter my mind; I was swearing on the floor. My haircut left and said good luck; I was really wishing it was one of my old ladies at that Moment, but he didn't know what to do.

In all the chaos the other 3 kids are scared and crying. I take Kimberly in my arms, blood-soaked, and she says, "Jesus Fix it Mommy". So, when anyone tries to tell me you can't learn from children I always beg to differ. I will give you angels the smooth landing.

I took all of us with blood-soaked Kimberly who was white as a ghost, to a walk-in clinic. The doctor took the three towels off I had on her. He gasped. That was very comforting...NOT! He told me to get to Bristol Hospital where a hand specialist would be waiting. When he had taken all the towels off, I saw that my Kimberly's ring finger and middle fingers on the left hand were half gone

In shock, I guess, I drove home and called Nancy the nurse, my friend who is Kristopher's Mom. I was not myself and she came quickly. Leah had gone to wait for her afternoon kindergarten bus on the front porch of blood. She came in and asked, "Mommy, can I please go to school?" I answered, "If the bus comes before Nancy, you can." Kimberly is getting whiter and quiet and heavy. Leah gives me these two things that look like grey erasers and says, "These are Kimberly's fingers". I put them on the counter and I hear the bus beep. Leah gives us each a kiss and Nancy is right behind the bus. She races in the house to see if Kristopher is okay, there is still blood everywhere. Nancy screams, "Get in my car!" As we're going she sees two grey things, and says, "I've got to get ice". While we're in the car now praying with Kimberly, Nancy hands me the plastic bag of ice.

When we got to the emergency at Bristol Hospital, Nancy burst through the doors and the hand doctor met us. Nancy cleaned the blood, called Douglas, and made herself into the clown "Sprinkles" for Kimberly. This memory is why my Kimberly wants to be a nurse.

For thirteen weeks we only prayed for those fingers. The doctor said Kimberly would have no fingernails or feeling in them. By faith she has nails on both fingers, not like her other fingers 'cuz these two are special. The teacher said she couldn't play violin, but she did from 2nd grade to high school. Kids always asked her why those two fingers looked different or funny, and she'd give them a faith lesson. Kimber, me, and the doctor who sewed the flaps of skin over her knuckles are the only three who saw them gone, except Jesus.

Kimberly is now twenty one. Kimberly is a dedicated daughter, incredible friend, and a faithful Christian. A virgin, she never drank or smoked, always stands up for what's right even when she stands alone. Now she is planning on going to nursing school, her heart's desire. She has her first boyfriend, which is why I say you will reap what you have sown. She has sown her seeds well, and God has blessed her greatly with a sincere man to reap with; a soul mate, if you will.

Kimberly has been my best friend, my closest angel, but seasons change. I can't wait to fly through this new season behind her, watching her wings grow and fly high.

Ecclesiastes 3:1 "To everything there is a season, and a time to every purpose under heaven".

I love you Bim!

PRODIGAL ANGEL

As I think of the Moments, the memories of my little Leah, they are all special. She was never my easiest child.

I remember crying to Douglas, thinking that my little girl hated me. I've done a lot of crying over this child. One day, she was so mad at me before she got on the school bus, that she slammed the door. It shattered the glass in the door. That day I prayed all day for my baby, and cried doing my customers. One of my older ladies told me that day that this one could end up being the closest to you when she gets older. Douglas always told me that Leah would be the closest to home, but I never believed him.

So we fly through my second baby, my first daughter, who inherited a bit of crazy from each of her parents. I'm sorry baby.

One of my favorite memories of Leah is the first note forged in school. It was in first grade, that's right 1st! She was in Mrs. Hammer's class who was the most awesome teacher. The note...I was a lot older when I

forged lots of notes. Looking back it's funny, but as a parent, not so much.

So, we jump to 11 years old, which is period time for my girls, and my Leah starts hers. I had talked to her already because I was so young and scared when I got mine and I didn't want my girls to be afraid. So, the next day I'm working in my salon when she comes to the door and motions for me. I go and she whispers, "Mommy I still have my period today!" Again, funny now, but at the time I felt terrible that I left out the time line for the menstrual cycle. Who does that?

My girl has always only wanted to be a wife and mother; that was always her desire. I remember in 7th grade, a teacher asked the class what they wanted to achieve in life. Leah's answer that day had been "a wife and mother". My little Leah was upset telling me about this cause the teacher answered her with, "You must want more than that." We talked for a long while that day as I explained how proud I was of that answer. I told her that day, "Those two things are the greatest and hardest work a woman can ever have."

The second church we attended introduced us to Camp Faithful which is where Leah met her first love. He was older than her, but I remembered what that was like. Eventually, he grows to be part of our family and a good friend of my oldest son. It was Leah and the boy, full speed ahead, for a long time. She planned her life around him. Time went on and this boy broke her heart after a few years.

Okay, so my little Leah was always extremely athletic and played all sports, but she really fell in love with softball and it became a huge part of her life. I don't know who loved softball more, Leah or Douglas watching her. At her last game she hit a home run, oh my...that was awesome! We have that ball!

Because of her strong love for Christ and that they offered softball Leah chose to attend a Christian college in Nyack New York. I think she thought it would be safe. I tried to tell her that a Christian school is made up of all kinds of kids. It doesn't mean everybody is like you. So she found out herself, had her experiences which I knew she would. We all need them to find our true angel inside, and so she flew. She loved her coaches, and they loved her. This is where she met Molly, who became DJ's girl!

At this time our family was having some church difficulties. DJ and Leah were drawn to a new Pastor, so we all went. His son and Leah were attracted to each other. Like me, boyfriends had always let her down. This could be "the One". The difference was this Pastor's son got the nerve to ask her to marry him and she said, "Yes". I have never seen my little girl so happy. However, her father and brothers were not happy at all. Only the girls in my house really loved this boy. I asked my daughter what the most important thing was to her about this boy? She said, "I know Mom, he will never ever hurt me. I trust him."

3 months before my life changing motorcycle accident, my Leah was married. My little girl paid for the entire wedding cause Douglas would not, hoping this boy would help. He did not. He was in the Navy so they both moved to Florida.

Then our accident happens. She came home 'cuz I was in the hospital trying to heal and so she had to talk to Douglas. He comes to my room and he's crying. He tells me of a nightmare experience this boy put my little girl through. Now, she doesn't want to go back. We talk her into it since you can't work on a marriage if you're not together. We sent her home to Florida. As parents, this was probably the most difficult thing we've ever done. So, she went.

This boy sent friends to pick her up and didn't care that his wife, and our family, were devastated. She told him she was pregnant and lost 20 pounds trying to work on a marriage alone. After that, Kimberly went to bring her sister home, still married and still praying for her baby's father.

Douglas and I watched our grandchild, Jayla Ann, be born. Kimberly cut the cord, and Molly coached Leah with my boys and extended family in the waiting room. When Jayla was born she looked *exactly* like her father; the Lord works in His own way. I think each of them have prayed she'll change. I knew she would 'cuz they all do. Now, she looks and laughs like a Malinowski. God is good.

Flying in fast forward, today is March 26. My little Jayla is 11 months old. I can't believe it! My Leah is in their room playing with her and they are laughing so hard. I know this 'cuz the monitor is still on in my room. These are priceless times for me.

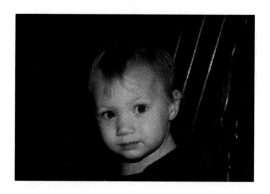

I'm writing the day after our littlest angel's 1st birthday. The whole family pitched in and the Lord arranged the beautiful weather. My Leah ordered everything Elmo. Jayla calls him "Melmo". Birdie, Leah's Godmother, made the most beautiful little cupcake just for Jayla to eat, and a fantastic Elmo cake for everybody else. Her crazy grandparents (US) got her the beginning Harley: an old fashion rocking horse, that's a pink rockin' Harley Davidson. A lot of people were there, lots of girls. Our littlest angel is blessed.

My oldest daughter, my little Leah has her dream, but not exactly how she or I had planned. The lessons she learned about life and herself were difficult to learn. We're all taught differently through our valleys of downward highways and our joys of quiet back roads. But learn we must angels.

Flying on, my girl is divorcing the boy who she thought would be a great Daddy, not an uncaring father. My girl is scarred but excited to start her life yet again, with much more information about herself, and her journey. We have become such close friends. Everything is so different now for us, since the accident, some for the better.

Watching her with her daughter is absolutely overwhelming. My prodigal angel has come home with a bundle of joy and finally now peace in her heart. I guess that the best reward a Mom has is watching her children be loving, caring, giving, and selfless parents.

Jeremiah 29:11-13 "The Lord declares He will not harm you. He will give you hope and a future. You will call upon Him and He will listen to you. You will seek Him and find Him. Seek Him with all your heart."

"Some things fall apart so better things can fall together."-Marilyn Monroe

Little Leah, love you!

CHANGEL

I'm upstairs in my room with the baby monitor, thinking of my oldest son. He is home down stairs, a rare event these days. He is in love and spends his free time with Molly, the way it should be.

My DJ was an extremely active child. He was walking at eight months. I remember the doctor telling me he would not have hand eye coordination since he didn't crawl enough.

I remember going to the park and such, people would look at him with sad eyes, probably thinking he had a growth problem 'cuz he was so tiny and walking.

DJ was always the kid at the beach you would have to watch every minute because he would just *go*. The water was his friend and he loved it. DJ was very little when Daddy first took him body surfing on his back. They were so much alike, physical athletic types; not like me. When DJ was three we were at a party. There was lots of drinking, as usual, and water. I remember people screaming, "The kid!" Douglas pulled DJ out of the water pounding on his back; then we could all three breathe again. As I look back on this young man's life, my first born, it overwhelms me.

DJ was four or five when his father took him for a ride on the motorcycle that we had at that time. I was sitting on the front porch as they rode by with DJ in the front, hands on the handle bars and his father leaning back on the sissy bar. That's right, **Douglas on the back.** I had a fit, which means nothing to my husband. *Large* anxiety Moment for me! Not my first, and definitely not my last.

He always wanted to play football. Since his birthday is February 3rd, his birthday parties moved to Superbowl parties after his long phase of being Donatello the ninja turtle. Now, at thirteen, he plays football. Any kid who has played football knows the hard work that's involved. Any parent who has driven to practice every night knows too.

At this point I need to give you little history. The first year my son played, the league's name was the Devils. Being a Christian DJ had a big problem with that. A devil head on his uniform for 2 years was a trial. We prayed for those two years that the name would be changed. It was the only league he could play in though, and play, he must. For two years DJ played for the Devils, and made weight.

This is a football story that is only a story because of prayer. The football league in our town before High School has a weight limit for each division. As they reach thirteen they grow, and grow but most kids make the limit before eighth grade. Well, DJ grew. Not fat, just tall and broad. At the first weigh in, he was 156 lbs but the weight limit is 140 lbs.

So, DJ began dieting and conditioning. His Dad (football maniac in his days) worked on the diet with him for encouragement! The willpower of this young man was definitely inspiring. DJ ate fruits and vegetables, *lots* of vegetables and was still singing around the house. He was driven to lose the weight. I was awestruck 'cuz as an adult my willpower was pathetic, but not his. After about 4 days my husband could not take it anymore; a burger is what took him down. But DJ, even without Dad continued on his mission. We prayed and asked God for help every night.

When DJ started eight grade I thought, "Oh no! The cafeteria would be rough for him." But not this young man. He ate Oatmeal in the morning, a juice box for lunch, and a salad or something for supper. I watched him each day in disbelief.

The church we were attending at the time was against him playing football at all, especially for a team named the Devils. They didn't believe in playing any sports really, anything to draw you away from the Lord. I agree with the concept, but the condemning attitude was too much. Since then we have left our church, after much prayer, seeking the Lord, and searching our hearts. And not for this reason alone, many others. My family and I thought all churches would be the same, separated, but that's not true.

So to get on with DJ story, we have found a new church. The pastor coaches and so does his wife. This was a big confirmation. There was to be no condemnation here. And so, football season begins. Our family had prayed so long about the name of this league, we'd sort of given up. This year, through prayer, DJ plays for the Colts! Now you many not think this is a miracle, but I certainly do. When my husband played before High School the league was, yes, the Colts! God did not forget our prayer, He heard, remembered and answered us, personally!

Now, another part of this is a girl named Leeann. She is 17, on fire for Christ and likes DJ a lot. They are the "count it all joy" kids. I introduce you to Leeann 'cuz she is a part of a day I will never forget.

A few weeks into dieting and training, the Colts had a scrimmage. I'm a hairdresser and scrimmages are on Saturdays, so Douglas goes 'cuz I'm working. My business is at home so that's where I was. Anyway, the phone rang and it was my husband. DJ was on his way to the hospital; it was his neck. His neck! My knees went weak. I began to cry, "My baby." Now I wanted him to just stop; gain weight, just stop playing.

I gathered my other 3 kids together to pray. While we prayed I thought of Leeann. I don't know why, but I did. My daughter went to call Leeann to pray and there was a knock at the door. It was Leeann. I couldn't believe it! The Lord definitely brought her there, just stopping by, for no reason. Just then my friend Debbie came by for a perm. So we have my 3 kids, Debbie and her 2 kids, Leanne, her brother and her Mom, all of us praying for DJ in my driveway.

Two hours later, which seemed like forever, my husband called. Every test had been done, and he's fine. Praise God!! Power of God through football!!

DJ is captain of the Colts. On the night before weigh-in he was still ¼ of a pound overweight. The next day, he clothed himself in a plastic bag sweatsuit, didn't eat a thing and left with Dad for the big weigh-in. Again, I was home working and waiting. DJ and I had prayed through this time a lot and now this was it. They pulled in the driveway, beeping the horn. DJ was glowing; he did it! The Lord had allowed him to just make it through. He weighed in at 140. Praise God!

The season will still be a sacrifice, one pound over and he couldn't play. Did I still want him to play football? No, not really, but I believe the Lord did. DJ was fighting a battle of choice. He wanted to play pro. The Lord was showing him what it takes: prayer, work, faith. The testimonies that have come from one young man's desire to play football amaze me.

In conclusion...

How important is football to my son? The bigger lesson for me was how important my son is to the Lord.

Fly through this with me to continue to get to know my oldest...

MY SON IS HIS SON

As he played football in high school, sang in the chorus, sang specials in church, his heart grew strong. He became part of a worship team, coached football, went to college, all with upstanding character. My boy is a unique upright spirit in a downtrodden world. He has been an angel to me more times than he could ever know. I know that my son will be a giving, loving husband, and a joyful teaching father.

As a Mom watching this life grow has been a joy beyond measure. His life will be a trip too, angels. I just hope I've made the bumps a little easier and fun! Our relationship has changed the most. That's why CHANGEL. After all, we prayed every morning together before school up into 11th grade.

DJ wrote his first song and sang it at church when he was seven. It is a gift. He's never stopped writing. His band is called the U.N.I.T.E.D – Unite Now In The Everlasting Deity- how proud could a Mom be? The song he wrote for the band's first CD is called

"Sunday Rebel"; that's him. He is a rebel for the cause of Christ.

All relationships go through low valleys and high mountains. Our relationship would be changed anyway because ...enter Molly. When my Leah brought her home from college, DJ already had a girl. Molly came to Leah's wedding when DJ had been broken by his girl. In time Leah's best friend became DJ's girl. When our accident happened, DJ had been following his dream of going to Tennessee to find his way. He came home when this our accident happened.

Since then Molly has moved here from California. My Leah lost her best friend to her brother but, in God's plan, is gaining a sister-in-law. My Changel has been blessed with the desire of his heart.

Here I give some history, to tell you how he proposed to his love. Molly was here when she got a call and became flustered. She said, "I will be back to tell you what happened." Later I learned the call was from a tattoo parlor telling her, her boyfriend was a bit woozy after getting a tattoo and needed to be picked up. So she went.

DJ & Molly
Malinowski

"Today I marry my friend. The one I laugh with, live for, love."

She entered and my boy was on bended knee with one bare foot out. On the top of it was tattooed, "Will you marry me?" How romantic! This Mommy is very proud of his romance and commitment. Molly's answering tattoo says, "Yes" with a huge diamond. When they put their feet together this tattoo becomes one. A beautifully written tattoo! This one event speaks volumes about my son's creativity, his commitment and his love. And what warms my heart is that the man's name who tattooed them is, yes, that's right, Angel!

God trusted me with my Changel because I would love and adore every quality of his character. It overwhelms me to know that I had a part of molding this character. As I watch from a distance the flight of my oldest the joy in my heart is unspeakable.

Psalm 33:3-4 "Sing unto Him a new song. Skillfully with a loud voice, for the word of the Lord is right, all His works are done in truth."

Donatello, Mommy loves you!

KIDS REPRESENT THE BUTTERFLIES IN MY GARDEN

Just as the caterpillar thought life was over she became a beautiful butterfly...

As a little girl I always loved babies. I babysat a lot and always wanted lots of kids. Douglas and I had talked about having 2-4-6-8 kids. He was very adamant about having an even amount of children. Me, I wanted a million. Having never recovered from the two abortions, and not being able to get pregnant right way, I was afraid. Then we talked about adopting and whala! After my fourth miracle child was born, and I think you can realize now that they are 4 true miracles, I was done. Kristopher was like my fifth kid; in my heart he always will be.

I absolutely loved hanging with my kids. It was my purpose. I had a customer that suggested that I consider foster care since I was patient with kids. Around the same time in church one Sunday, a woman told me she had a word from the Lord for me. She told me that many, many children would call me Mom. I told her that I'd had my tubes tied after my fourth baby. She said, "I can't tell you why, but many, many will call you Mom". Douglas felt our children were too young to begin fostering more. He decided we should wait until they were older, so I let it go.

In those years however, not all the kids in my life called me Mom. But boy have I loved many, many kids as one. Our children have been brought up with me always loving everyone. Even now if I say I love them my kids say, "It doesn't matter, Ma. You love everybody." Now reading this they will understand how and why I can love the unlovable.

Here we fly through fostering. To me this meant eventually getting a kid back to their Mom. We entered a class to get our license for specialized foster care; these were kids with heavy baggage.

We begin with an adorable six year old who had been through unspeakable things. I would rock him to sleep. My kids and all the kids in and out of our house loved him 'cuz he was little and cute. Through many trials we fostered him back to his Mom. It was rewarding, and I wasn't sure his wings were ready, but the decision was out of my reach.

Enter our David. Some memories with David are lights on the path of my trip. He came to us at nine years old, and decided to leave at almost eighteen. David endured much with our family. Our family endured much with our David. I pray always for his wings. We love you.

Psalms 91:11 "He shall give His angels charge over thee and keep thee and all thy ways."

Another young man came to us for a three day vacation from his foster family. We fought to keep Scotty. He came at twelve and on May 16, 2010 was twenty-one. He is an angel who likes to put past baggage in the past. Not all of us are able to do this.

I've watched this flight of ups and downs always balance out in the end. Like a butterfly he always tries the best he can. My Scotty has a girl now, her family, a job and school. We talk through music now you have to dance out of the cocoon of our family.

So, be careful with those wings my boy. Oh, so many memories to take with you on your flight. Love you when you're gone.

Jude 1:24 "Unto Him that is able to keep you from falling, to present you blameless with exceeding joy."

In the midst of these two there were two more. Trials had heaped on them too young, wings older then they should have been. There comes a time you have to let go because the student is not hearing the teacher. We tried, we prayed, they chose to go. Only so many feathers can be plucked from your wings until your flight is hindered. My hope is that they both fly. I pray they both listen to your gentle voice inside. Let hope keep you through your flights. They each have a piece of my heart.

Try to remember angels; don't run from life, fly toward it.

1 Peter 5:7 "Cast all your cares upon Him for He cares for you."

DAYS
WITH
DAD

The very first memories I have of my Dad are at the Drive-In. It was like part of our family; the most important part.

I was little when I went to Boston a few times with Daddy. When it was just me and him it felt special. He always talked to me like I was grown up. He made me feel important. And I always had to get dressed up to go to Boston. It was a big deal. It required a dress, laced bobby socks, patent leather shoes and a purse with a pencil and pad of paper. He'd explain to me what would happen inside the big brick building. The men all went in a big office and I stayed in the outer office with the Secretary, I think her name was Betty. I could hear the men yelling inside their office, but Betty would give me little jobs and I loved that.

On the way home we'd go out to lunch, sometimes with the other men and sometimes it was just us. My Dad always got me a Shirley Temple. I guess so I felt like a grown up. He always ordered for me whenever we went anywhere. I never got my guts up to say I liked Coke a Cola better. Way back then drive-in's had to bid for their movies from the outer office. So, on the ride home he'd tell me the movies he'd won. I loved those days.

A huge memory for me of my Dad is when my brother Arthur left for Vietnam. I had never seen Daddy cry before. It was very difficult for our small family unit! My mother wore a black dress for a year, but my Dad went on like normal. Looking back now, he was actually hyper-normal.

When the Drive-In burned down and we rebuilt it, I was with Daddy a lot. He told me I was like his gopher; Dad's kind of joke... go for this, go for that. He always made me feel like I was helping him.

So, in short my Dad made my problems just "go away" I guess, never to be spoken of again.

My Mom was getting sicker and weaker. She landed in the hospital. This is what I think finally changed my Dad toward Douglas. Douglas came to the hospital almost every day with me. He would talk to her even though she wasn't always making sense and Daddy would watch him. Douglas was great with my Mom, and that was great for Daddy. After six months of this, my Mom passed away on April 10, 1980. I had told my Dad I was so tired, and it was the one night I wasn't there.

When my Dad called to tell me, I was alone and my Dad didn't know that. All I remember is Douglas getting me out of our bedroom closet. I just lost it. Then, the whole wake, funeral, oh my goodness. At this time in my life I blamed God for all this.

Dad dealt with it. He told me to come over and help him clean out. When I got there, he had a ½ gallon of Seagrams and 1 bottle of Gingerale. We proceeded, I guess, to remove my Mom so he could move on. We were drunk to say the least and I searched for letters everywhere; letters my Mom had told me about when I was thirteen. Letters that she said Pat, my birth mother, had written. I looked from the attic to the basement and through everything Daddy was throwing out. The letters were nowhere to be found; nowhere, and I'm telling you angels, I searched. Drunk, of course, I had the courage to ask my Dad about them. With a non-expression he said, "Those have been gone for years". So I gave up.

I took her jewelry and jewelry box, 'cuz she and I would play with the jewelry in it all the time. I saved a few things I knew were her mother's and some sentimental stuff my Dad would have thrown out.

I missed my Mom more when I had each of my kids. Even though Daddy did okay, my Mom would have been incredible with them.

After my Mom had been gone, maybe three months or so, he called. He asked how I'd feel if he'd went out dinner with Agnes. She was the ticket lady for 100 years at the Drive-In with him, so I have known her forever. Her husband had died soon after my Mom. He asked me what people would think. I said, "Who cares if you want to go, go." He asked me how I'd feel. I asked, "Do you want to go?" He said, "Yes". So, he went. They were together, not married, in separate houses, 'til she passed. These two were older yet very healthy and on the go. And boy oh boy they went. They went on cruises and trips. They knew a lot of the same people since they had worked together forever. Our families knew each other already which made it that much easier. They did things together they could not do with their mates. I'm so happy they had that companionship.

Now they worked up until my Dad was eighty-five. I don't know exactly how old Agnes was, but close to that. My girls cleaned my Dad's house for him and Douglas and the boys were doing maintenance stuff around the house and the Drive-In. Then Agnes passed away. My Dad went every day to see her, and then he lost her.

This next part is probably the hardest for me. As I cry, you fly through the dark journey with glimmers of heavenly light on this trip.

Near the end of my father's life, a time where I know Jesus, we talked. I knew him better after his passing then I ever did while he was with me here. One thing he told me, among many others, was that he loved his Gram-ma more than anything. His own mother and father had gotten divorced in 1915. (That's right angels, before it was "normal" practice.) He told me he never knew his Dad, his mother worked at the market in town and he was with his Gram-ma a lot who took him to church. She had taught him about Jesus. He was fixing organs, lighting church lights and helping her make communion wafers when he was very young. I don't know if you can imagine my shock, finding out my Dad went to church very young, as I clean his teeth in the sink 'cuz he'd only let me do it. He also told me about a dream of how he used to go to a rock and pray to Jesus.

Around this time, Daddy would only eat if I fed him. He would pretend he was sleeping if someone came to see him, then squeeze my hand when they were gone. He knew I couldn't help laughing, I think that's why he did it.

We held hands every day, just like when I used to travel to Boston with him. We shared SO, so many family secrets, feelings he had, and love; priceless to my heart. I believe I saw how he truly felt which I don't believe he shared with anyone. He told me one day I was *his* Angel! That was the ultimate. I also think it was that same day he asked me to clean up after he moved his bowels. Never in my life did I see *that* coming. He didn't want the nurse, he wanted me. Thank God I was there for him. By now, his butt was the size of a baby's butt. When I turned him back over, I wiped a tear from his eye, and his terrible, dry, no- teeth mouth and said, "I'm sorry".

I remember so well when Douglas, Arthur, or his other son Frank would come in. He'd try to sit up and be the strong man he always was. It was getting to the point that I had to interpret for him 'cuz no one else could understand his sign language or his words.

One of these times he asked me to go home and get some socks for him. I told him, "You have the nice warm hospital ones Daddy", but he shook his head no. He was showing me he wanted his black ones from home, the silky ones pinned in pairs with a safety pin. As I get older, I think my Daddy had the most important angel wings in my life, and boy did he fly. So I felt I was being Daddy's Angel for the first time in my life. Of course I went to get silky black socks for him. And that's when my own wings stopped flying for what seemed like year. My wings felt cut off. The letters my Mom had told me about were there among the socks in Daddy's drawer. I had been in that drawer at least a million times. I was in that drawer for my Dad the day he went to the hospital, they weren't there. Even now I don't know how they got there.

All I cared about was reading every single one, so I did. I think my heart actually exploded that day 'cuz my Daddy Angel gave me the last gift he could. In heaven maybe, angels, my Dad wanted me to read the letters after he was gone...he controlled this event. He knew his life journey was ending. I read those letters through many tears.

PARTS AND PIECES
OF PATRICIA

June 13, 1958
Friday Noon

Dear Dad,

I hope this letter finds you
in the best of health. I am O.K.

I've wanted to write a long
time ago, but I just couldn't write
the words. Now I guess I can
find the words. I some how feel
~~and~~ know Dad that the cards &
money sent to me on my
birthday were all sent by you

is something that keeps us
apart. It's life itself, I guess.
You really know very little
about me. Don't you? You
can't deny it Dad. As I myself know very little about you.
I guess we were not meant
to be together, that's why we
know so little. My words
may sound puzzling but I
hope you'll understand me
just this once.

There is one thing I want
you to know Dad. Father's
Day in it self is a special
Day for Father's, but to me

→

132

3.

it's a different day. It's a day
I wish I had a father to
be with me. I some how know
Dad, you love me in your own
way, and I love you too very
much. This letter is well, a
so-long letter to you Dad. I
wish with all my heart that
you, Marge and Art, find all
the happiness in the world.
I feel you no longer need
letters from me, because I
always say the wrong things.
But Dad, promise me, you'll
never forget me. I only
wish you and I could
←

133

(4)

have been real, father &
Daughter. Of course it's done,
and well I guess it's all
over. I'm sorry sometimes
for things I say, but
mostly to me, they mean
something.

Dad, Good Luck in all you
do, and God Bless You.

Remember, me, and I'll
always remember you.

"Happy Fathers Day"
"To a Father I Love."

"Your Only Daughter"
"Loving Daughter"
"Lasting Love"
"Always,"
"Pat"

November 15, 1958
Thursday Noon
Time : 4:00 P.M.

Dear Dad, Mum, & Art,
     Hope this letter finds you all
feeling good. As for myself I am
quite well.
     To start off may be you'll
be interested in knowing that I'm
getting married. I'm also going
to have a baby. I'm 3½ months

May 15, 1959
Monday

Dear Mum, Dad, + Art.

Sunday I received your telephone call and was ever so glad to hear you. Gosh Mum, I wanted to tell you on the phone about Mother's Day, but Mr. Dousette was right there and well I didn't feel so comfortable with him listening to me, like he was. I'm fact I didn't care for it at all. But oh well! Mum, I know when you was here Thursday and spent the day, we talked and had swell time. Then I should of gotten you something for Mother's Day. While I had the money. After all you've done for me, and I didn't even send a card or any thing. Believe it or not Mum, I feel so darn bad, and I know deep down inside you feel hurt to Mum, your the last person in the whole world I want to hurt, and it seems I always do hurt you. Mum, now I'm older and a lot wiser, I've realized a lot, and understand a lot of things

→

136

you tried to tell to me and help me
so much. Mum, I want you to know
I love you very much, and may be
some day I can prove it to you. I
Remember you always told me, that
gifts and the such, never really showed
love, so may be a few words will
show a little of my love for you.
Mum, you've always done right by
me, and tried so hard to make me
grow up right. Mum, you haven't
failed me at all, not even through
all my selfishness and meaness. You
always stayed right there pitching in.
Mum, from the bottom of my heart,
and as a woman, I'm proud of
you, and I love you, as only a
daughter can love her mother. Thank
you Mum, for just being you. Never
stop pitching Mum. Your a Peach.
   I'm sorry to hear your not
feeling to good Mum. Please take
it easy and try not to worry
                                    →

about any-thing. I sure hope the baby is born soon (Gwen Marie will be in all her glory when she comes out. I think she's trying a little harder each day to come. Hope she hurries a little. She sure kicks good and proper. Tonight I go to the Dr's again. Gosh seems like I was just there yesterday. Well, I think I'll leave the letter for a bit and clean a little, and then go to see the Dr. once again. I'll continue this letter as soon as I return from the Dr's office. It's only a little wait, so don't go away. Be back shortly.

Well, here I am again. It wasn't to long was it. Well. the Dr... is sure I'll have the baby by this week end, because of the location of $\rightarrow$

the baby's head. Gosh, the way my belly hurts right now, I swear it is coming real soon. Hurts a little when I walk. Gosh, I hope Gwen Marie will come fast & easy. I think she's had enough fun already. Oh, gosh I'm so excited as the time comes nearer & nearer. Still seems hard to believe I'm going to be a mother. I know and feel like a million. Every one is so anxious for the baby to come, and if they only knew how anxious I am. Gosh, since the date was by this week, the baby should be here, I can't wait. I was so afraid at first, but, so help me I'm not now. Of course I have no idea how I'll act when the labor pains get real bad. I only hope I have courage to not yell, like a lot do. I guess with the first one every mother wonders how she'll react to her pains. I know I'll try hard, and push with every pain. The only thing Dr. Thompson gives the mother is ether, only a little, while in delivery. He feels to many things will make a groggy baby and will cause the mother to be laid up to long. I sure hope I'm not boring you with all my thoughts. I want you not to worry, and while in labor I'll think of you and I know every-thing will be O.K. Mum, you always gave me courage. You put a good back bone in me, I'll put it to good use just for you.

Well, I guess I've run out of words, so I'll make like a door and close for now.

Stay as sweet as ever, and

→

140

I'm always thinking of you.

Take care of your selves, and I love you.

Sonny sends his best and hopes to see you soon.

Remember Maam, keep on Praying and keep the faith.

"Lasting Love"
Pat
Sonny
+
"Gwen Marie"
Scott Brian

P.S. Thanks so much for calling. I was never so glad to hear from you. Love, kisses + Loads of Prayers.

With glasses my Mommy Angel is hugging her step-daughter, Patricia, my birthmother. I'm still in awe of finding this picture of my "Moms" together.

July 6, 1959

Dear Dad Buzzell

Just a few lines to
tell you that Pat and I are
coming for the bably, Dad why
don't you and mun like me,
is it because you think that
I am not good for her - Well
maybe you think different when
you read is, They are a few thing
you heard, but they are not trut,
Dad I like you and mun, very
much, but you don't even want
to give me and Pat a chance.
Pat is my wife, and she know
right from wrong, I want so much
to give her thing, but nobody
want to help me get started,
I have a wonderful wife, and
she need me so much, you probly
think she deserve some one better,
I think she got some one, she
love and that a lots. Dad

143

I know right from wrong, and
may be you think that I haven't
got what it take, but I have.
Dad please understand, I love
your Daughter and won't ever
let her down, I haven't got
much to offer, but what I have
got I intent to keep what I
have – Dad I never had anything
but when your daughter came
into my life, she done a lot
for me, please don't try to make
her go against me, Dad what I
done to make you and Mun hate me
it make me feel hurt when I know
Some one don't like me, Will you
please tell me what it is, because
I want to know, and corect it,
and also I love the bably very
much, and want to care and take
it off your hand.

Dad please give me a chance
to proof my love for Pat and
baby, I think you must know
that the Gwen isn't mine, but
for give me will you, Pat is very
much in love with her and want
to bring her up, I do to.
Please try to understand me
will you. I don't want to
have you hate me, I want so
much for you and mun to like
me, Please give me and Pat
a chance, ~~thank you~~ Thank You
very much — God Bless You

                        Pat and Son

Sept 19

Hi Dad

Just a few lines
to tell you that Pat
has left me, Dad do
you know that we can't
do any thing with out
Gwen, Every body think
that Pat is no good because
of her talking the bably
down to you, we want the
bably back, if you was
any kind of a father, to
her, you would help her,
and me, If the bably was
mine may be thing would
be different, but it isn't
so I am trying to be a
father, but you and your
wife wan't let me. Dad

②

please help Pat, She
is sick and need some
thing to grow up with,
I want to be a father
of Gwen, Please help me
to get her back, that
what she need, I will
work my fingers to the
bones for her, Dad do you
know what you are doing
to her and I. Pat want
to be a mother. I want
her back please, Every night
she dream of her and she
doesn't care if she live
or die. Dad I know that
I don't meet your class
classification, but you
think that I can't take
care of Pat and Gwen,
well I can, why don't

②

do you put us to a
test and find out,
if you did that then
you would be thinking
of Gwen and Pat, when
you read this letter, plea
don't forget you were
a father once, (remember
or don't you? I want
Pat back and you have
to give her a chance to
proof her love for Gwen
and me, Dad please
help me, thank you
for reading this letter
and God bless you.
I love Gwen no matter
what,

Your Turfy
Sonny Rufy
PS I work for Fifth Ave Shoe)

148

Oct 5, 1959

Dad Buzzell
          I am writing this
letter to tell you, That we
are coming down for my baby,
and if you think that you
can stop me, you go on and
try, I so fled up with everyone
telling me what to do, I am
not going to Court, and you
better have her ready for me
because I will be down, and
you tell your wife, that if
she try and stop me I will
have her arrested for forcing
my wife, into getting a divorce
she remembers, all the week
that she was up here, she
talk about me, making my
wife cry. I was so glad

149

when she left, I admit ~~my f~~ one thing Dad, I ~~think~~ you was pretty nice, and ~~think do~~, still do, I don't ~~you life~~, like your wife, but she doesn't like me, Dad, I love Pat and the baby, she is the only thing, I ever love, and the baby she is a dream - Dad why does everyone hate me, ~~it~~ is it because I haven't got money like some people who I know, I haven't got look but that skin deep, When ~~you~~ try to get Pat down to Conn, and she said that I wasn't welcome, you make me hurt, Dad don't take my baby away from us, I want to be a father to it, and

(3)

bring her up, so I can be
proud and look up to it
and say the Sam she thing. Dad please
don't take it away from us,
I will take care of her, just
give me a chance, to proof
my faith in God and Pat,
All my life things have been
taken away, please don't
do this to me and Pat,
Don't you know what you are
doing, you are hurting Pat,
You should seen the look
on her face, she was very
happy, I was very proud
of her, what she wont though
she make me very happy,
Dad I will be down to
get the baby and going
to get Pat, and come down
and Get Gwen Marie

Mr. + Mrs. Richard T. Buzzell
24 Red Oak Drive
Forest Hill Park
Plainville, Connecticut

Dear Dad, Mum, Art & Gwen Marie,

Hope this letter finds you all in the best of health. As for my-self I just fine.

You called and asked for the picture of Art, but Dad & Mum, when I left Sonny in Thornhill. He packed everything in boxes at his mother's house and I've looked high and low for the picture, but I can't find it. In fact all the pictures I had are gone. Sonny said he packed them all, but they are not in any of the boxes. I shall ask Fairlee if she had them or if she put them somewhere. ok.

Was glad to receive your call and to once again hear out how Gwen is. Dad and Mum I wish to never again hear from you. I realize it's not right to say what I'm about to say, but, it's for every-one's good. Ever since I brought the baby to you. I know what I've done to my-self I gave away the one thing in life that I ever really loved. But as you know it is to late, as it is always been. I never did think before I did something.

You see Dad & Mum, I can't ever face you again, I am ashamed and hurt, and feeling sorry for my self. I need nothing to remind me of the baby, because I have my mind, and my dreams. I even hate to go to bed any more. First she's big, then she's a baby, then she's old, but she's always there. I see a baby some where, or the women at Profile talk of their baby's and the feeling is there. I can't explain the feeling, for there is no words to express it. Once again Pat fails at something, once again Pat takes away good-ness, and once again feels sorry for her self. Same old Pat. Did you ever hate your-self, well, I hate my-self.

There is nothing you or anyone can do for me I know, for I've made my bed, now I have to lay in it. May-be some day when I begin to grow up, I'll realize or think a bit different. I'm only 19 and I've never done any-

thing right, except to give life to a
beautiful baby girl. That's all, and to
top it off, I took her away. I always
deserve what I got. You only get out of
life what you put in it.

You'll never know how I feel inside, never as long as you live. I have
to live my self, and my guilty concious.
Some times may be it'll get the best of me,
or I'll conquour it.

I took off from Haverhill, I ran
away as usual, but I'm not going to
run any more. I'm tired of running.
The only thing I was running from was
my self. Running won't help me, I
know that.

I went to Portsmouth, and stayed
with the Willis for awhile, and then
moved to Everett St. with Judy &
Kenny. Then moved to 46 Portland St.,
where I am now. Remember when you
sent the telegram to me, for me to
call you, well I called that and
two days later, I took Sonny with

4

me. There again is something you'll
never understand. So he's not hand-
some, or smart, and can't spell so good.
But he's helped me and loved me.
Even though I walked out on him
and we were separated for more than
2 months, I always thought about him
and missed him. He is with me
now for ever, and I've found a
little happiness which has been
missing. Sonny means a lot to me.

I know you care Elsie of what Sonny and I are doing, but, I wanted you to know we are trying to get back on our feet once again. The road is quite bumpy but, it will smooth over in time.

I'll never as long as I live ever return to Haverhill, Mass. I am a coward to face anyone. Doesn't much matter, ma gave me up a long time ago, now she needn't ever have to see me again. She is well rid of me.

Can you read between all the words that I've written. May be you can. I'm all twisted up inside, I'm a bundle of trouble. Back on Mass. there is nothing for me but

This is probably one of those letters you won't understand so try to understand.

It is a letter I wish for you to know, it is the very last one. I've broken your hearts, and I've broken own. It is high time I stopped and let you go your own roads.

I want to see you, yes, but where Sonny isn't welcome neither am I. You see, he is my husband, I took marriage vows to love him, and to honor, and that is what I'm doing. I need Sonny and he needs me.

I so wanted to come to Connecticut to see Gwen, but I can't do it. —

I don't know what year but it's the only picture of my birthmother and I. To me she was my sort of sister. After reading her letters I cannot imagine how she felt. Thank you, Jesus for moving my Dad to give me that last gift. After reading all of them over and over, I went to the hospital to say thanks. My Dad turned his head away, put up his hand and never spoke of his only daughter's letters to her Dad about me.

It was a conversation about the rock. I asked him if he could see angels there. He shook his head. I asked, "Do you really see Jesus?" and he shook his head yes. I told him that day to stay at the rock, don't come back.

"What do you have to let go?" He just pointed at me. So I said "Daddy, you gave me my letters. You are my only Dad. I miss you already, but let go I will be okay." He put his hands up and walked with his fingers. I asked him if he wanted me to go. He answered slowly whispering with his pathetic dry toothless tiny mouth, "You walk." We did this three times. I'd go for a walk, pray and go back to him and after the third time he whispered, "It's not working." He was trying to punch his own ticket to heaven. I told him with my last kiss, I would see him tomorrow. He shook his head no.

The next day was the call, June 3ʹ 2004. I thought it was the worst day and the best all at one time. I was the one who told him he'd be healed in heaven, hallelujah. But for this Angel-in-training, it was awful. I never realized how much I would miss him 'til he was gone. Douglas and my kids were my strength.

When we went to the funeral home my Dad had taken care of it all. Even the flowers were to be taken to the rehab places where my Mom, and then Agnes died. He tried to control his time of death like he controlled everything and everyone. But, God's timing is always perfect. Now, since the motorcycle accident, I believe he had to be taken so he wouldn't have to endure my pain with me. He missed his 90th birthday by three months. He was blessed with a long life.

I can't wait to be greeted in heaven by my Mom or Daddy and his daughter, my mother. That's my hope as I fly on...

Eternal Love

Richard T. Buzzell
Died June 3, 2004

Time is.....
Too slow for those
who wait,
Too swift for
those who fear,
Too long for
those who grieve,
Too short for
those who rejoice,
But for those
who love.....
Time is Eternity

Newington Memorial Funeral Home
20 Bonair Avenue
Newington, Connecticut

NO TIME

Angels, if you have something to say, try to say it because sooner than you think there may be no time. This much I've learned.

Angels, going back a little further, here's a huge **Moment**. At 36 years old my **father called to tell me Patricia died. Taking a** minute to figure out who that is, I said, "What happened?" **He** told me he wasn't quite sure, **but**, Frank (his son, Pat's brother) **had called him to tell him when the funeral was. My father then began to explain to me that** Patricia's mother would be coming for the **funeral. I asked my Dad if he wanted to go. He** said, "I will go if you want to." I said, "Do you want me to?" **This is not dysfunctional at all.** So, we go. He goes for me, I go for him.

The morning comes and my father's **girlfriend, Agnes, is coming too. In the car we have my** father "birth grandfather", **and his girlfriend in the front. In the back seat, we have me and m**y grandmother, who I don't **remember meeting. She flew in from Florida** for her only daughter's funeral. **My birth**

 grandfather and my grandmother are now going to their only daughter's funeral. I can't quite put it into words how

bizarre this "trip" to Massachusetts was because my father and his girlfriend are in the front seat talking about where they are going to lunch and my grandmother, in the back seat with me, has a box of pictures of Patricia as a little girl.

Okay angels, I'm in the back with my grandmother who I don't know at all. She explains to me how she hasn't spoken to Patricia since she had me. At 36 I'm looking at pictures of my birthmother when she was little for the first time. Remember angels, with the grandmother that I don't know. I laugh now, I didn't then. She was telling me pieces of Patricia when she was little. As I think back comparing the picture of Pat to my face, both faces about the same age, how could I be adopted? If you remember angels, I told everybody I was picked special.

I thought to myself, "God forbid, that this would ever happen to me and my children. My wings would shatter."

In the 36 years of my journey this two-hour drive was the longest two hours of my life. As we drove, my thoughts wandered back to another funeral when my adopted Mom had passed away. I couldn't help feeling a bit sorry for myself, that at 36 I'd lost two mothers.

I thought back even more to a day my Mom and Dad took me to meet Daddy's daughter from his first marriage. I must have been close to 7 years old. I asked Mom all kinds of questions that day. By the time we got to Pat's house I knew she had 3 kids, blonde hair, was chubby (like me) and she laughed a lot. In my little mind I already knew I loved her, she was sort of my sister. I remember my Dad being real quiet that day, just like this trip.

164

We pulled into a driveway much different from ours at home. It was scary. We walked up a few steps and a chubby short smiling lady came to the door. Greeting me with a bear hug, I knew this was Pat. Walking into the kitchen I remember three highchairs.

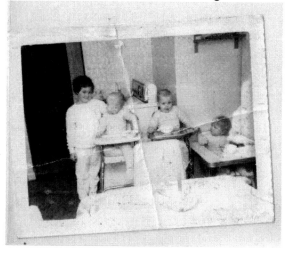

The kids looked like triplets. My Mom told me they were 4, 3, and 2. My Dad wasn't saying much. Now I know why; he was very uncomfortable. Pat talked and giggled, my Mom cried, which was very out of character for my Mom. When I asked her what was wrong, she said she was just happy for us to meet.

I also remember thinking Pat and her kids were much different from our family. Their highchairs were old, their clothes were old and their faces were dirty. I didn't have anything old, and I don't ever remember being dirty. My Dad was doing his soft whistle thing, which means he was ready to go. I felt an ache in my belly, I didn't want to go. Pat gave me a huge hug. Still giggling, she told me she loved me. We said goodbye and left. As young as I was, I knew that for the two hours to get there, and two hours home, we hadn't stayed long.

As I drove with my Dad to Pat's funeral, I remembered the day my Mom told me I was adopted and that Pat was my birth mother. A 13 year old kid had changed that day. Why did Pat keep the other 3 kids? Did she just not like me? I had felt lied to, betrayed. All the memories came rushing back. As I sat in the car for the ride that seemed endless, my confusion was compounded.

We get to the funeral home; my father is in prime denial mode. I get out of the car and see my two half-siblings, Keith and Scott. They come to hug me. After losing my mother, I knew how they felt. My heart was breaking for them. As I walked in behind my father and his girlfriend, my grandmother was walking behind us. She hugged the boys quick and kept on walking. They didn't know who she was either.

We all signed the book. I remember my father signed his name; no Dad, just his name. I walked in and the first person I saw said to me, "You must be Gwen". I thought to myself, "How could you possibly know that? I don't know who you are." But, what I said was, "Yes, I am". She said, "I loved your mother. She was a wonderful person." That's when I knew that Pat had talked about me. Just knowing that angels, healed my heart a bit.

Going around the corner I saw the casket, and a woman kneeling in front of it. My father and his girlfriend walked by, looked and then sat down. I went and kneeled down, and realized that the woman was my half-sister, Kelly. She was crying. I put my arm around her, and she said to me, "She would be so glad you're here". My heart broke for her 'cuz I had lost my mother too, but not today; today it was *her* Mom. Today, what *I* lost, was a mother I never knew. I never saw Patricia face to face as mother and daughter. So many things I wanted to ask and have answers to. And now no time!

As I looked at her in the casket, it was like looking at myself. I looked more like her than all three of her other kids. It came back to me why my father would yell, "Patricia!" to me when he was mad. Pat had a big rhinestone pin that simply said, "Jesus". Angels, that seemed to make it okay that I had no time; Jesus was there. He reminded me of that with a simple rhinestone pin. I asked Kelly if her mother knew the Lord, and she said yes.

As I got up to go sit down, there was a huge floral arrangement that said "Love, Mom & Dad". I thought, "Wow", they really did care. I told my father, "Your flowers are beautiful." He said, "They are not from us". I said, "Well, then who?"

As the day went on people kept coming up to me, asking me if I was Gwen. One of the women told me after that she and her husband were like a mother and a father to Patricia. She said to me, "After her parents died, she became very close to us." I asked her, "Are those flowers from you?" She said "Yes"

In this bizarre road of my trip, trying to cope with having no time left at my birth mother's funeral, I looked at my father's face hearing this news. His daughter had told people that he was dead. I wonder now if he thought, there's no time. No time for him to know his daughter, no time for his daughter to know him.

My half-brother comes to my father and says, "Grandfather, I need to talk to you". He took my father into another room, and he asked Frank to join them. I followed. To help you follow this trip of mine, Frank is Patricia's brother. That's right, my Uncle. So, this is his father with his nephew and me, his niece. None of us know each other at all...okay...travel on angels.

Keith proceeded to ask my father, and Frank, to give him money toward the funeral. My father, in his stern manner, dismissed it. Keith still tried, but it was done. My father was done at this funeral!

I still wanted to know how she died. I chose Scott the quiet one to ask. He told me that she had a gastric bypass, and after many complications, she died. My mind went back to the car with my grandmother looking at the pictures of Pat when she was little. My grandmother mentioning quite a few times, "She was chubby, just like you." So angels, chubby was a huge thing to Patricia. She went to great lengths to have surgery to change it, and died doing it.

My father was already in the car with his girlfriend and my grandmother, probably talking about where they were going to lunch again. All waiting for me, Kelly and the boys wanted a picture. I went outside after answering a few more people asking me if I'm Gwen and a few other people asking me if I ever found out who my "real" father was. One of the women there thought that it was her son. After explaining to this woman that I was there with Patricia's father, she said, "I thought he was dead". So, I tried to explain to her that he was in the car waiting, and he never did that well. I felt like I had no time to say the things that I wanted. No time to talk to this new person who thought her son was my father... no time.

My half-brother Keith comes to me and says, "I'm sorry for everything I did to you. Your husband must want to kill me. Is that why he didn't come with you?" I said, "Thank you for your apology, and be glad that he didn't come with me." Then the three kids that I remember in high chairs, me, and another woman that I don't know stood in front of the funeral home for a picture.

Now I get in the car after saying my good byes and my father says to his first wife, my grandmother, "Are you glad you came for that?" I don't remember her answer but it was quick. That was the last thing ever said about that funeral. Then we went to lunch.

Driving the two hours back home, I don't remember my grandmother saying anything. My father and Agnes were in the front seat talking about the Drive–In and such. I was wishing that I hadn't waited until there was no time. No time to know my birth mother, no time to talk to the people at her funeral about her, no time to know my half siblings.

I asked the Lord to help me through this strange second mother pain, and he did! The way that was best for me. In my character, no matter how bad things are, or how confused I may become, my cup is always half full, never half empty. So, to look for the crumb of joy in this day, that was it! Just knowing that HE is there for me no matter where I am, whether I am looking for HIM, or not. It doesn't change the fact that He is always there.

Angels, try not to learn the hard way. That whatever time you are in, try to make the most of it. It's different for all of us; our "trips" can't all be the same. There are people that we journey with, as I did in this car, that sometimes need to hear from our heart. Try not to leave yourself with no time.

The ride home was weird but the Lord spoke to my heart that day. I've never felt bad about any of it since. The Lord showed me that I have the Dad he wanted me to. I would never hurt my Dad for anything. I had two Moms who loved me so much. One conceived, gave birth

and picked out my parents. The other Mom
molded me. I thank God for both of my Moms.
But most of all I thank Him for a rhinestone pin
that simply said, "JESUS".

FELLOW FLYERS

So now angels we fly through help I've given and pieces of myself that have been taken.   Balance is a characteristic I don't have, or so I've been told. You can judge for yourself.

If you remember in the beginning of my trip my Mom talked to me about belly friends, the friends who come over for the snacks and pool. I guess that was the beginning of my becoming a "usee". To explain, a "usee" it is the opposite of a user. Users are traveling on a different plateau then we the "usees". They find me on the well-lit terrain and on the dark paths. Their compass, map, or whatever they use directs them to ME. So in the beginning were the belly friends and I loved them all. Then I became a taxi and I loved it. Somewhere in the middle I was a boy/man pleaser. In some of the travels I became an abusee, opposite of an abuser. Later a substitute Mom, counselor, lender, doting wife, caterer, teacher, etc...etc...etc...

I have to say I have always been generous. As a hairdresser for thirty years if I

174

had been paid for every head I've done I'd be rich! I have been known to barter for drugs or whatever someone else needed to deal for. I have been paid in meatballs, scratch tickets that lost, food stamps, a book someone thought I should read, babysitters that never sat. And then there have been the friends who I suppose I never expected to pay me.

I can say without a doubt I have been a good friend. Other things in my character I've failed but friendship is not one. Because I'm searching for myself I believe I now understand why. Being raised with a brother who was thirteen years older with no sisters and no cousins, my friends became my family. This part of me doesn't really think, it just feels. The friends who I consider true friends now are much fewer than I ever thought they'd be. Many people will come and go in your life. I fully believe each of them come for a reason and go for a reason.

My Mom brought me up to treat people how I want them to treat me, so I always have. Imagine my surprise, and I remember this clearly, when I found that in my Bible. The golden rule…"Do unto others as you would have them do unto you."

Although angels, I can say, I have loved like Jesus. I know this 'cuz it's painful. When anyone hurts, I hurt. I can't explain it really; it's a mystery. As a result of this, I get used and abused and must count that as joy. One trait of mine that has always held true is, J.O.Y…Jesus-Others-Yourself. Before I met Jesus I guess for me it was OY! ….Others- Yourself. I've been called a people pleaser over and over on my trip and that's ok.

Some of my memories will have to stay inside my brain damaged head. We've had such an extended family made up of all different people, so get your wings ready as we fly on.

- ❖ The Bristol youth group, where I left a large piece of my heart, I still pray for each of your flights. You're all angels. I pray you fly carefully.
- ❖ Each Pastor we've had has taught us very differently, 'cuz each of us have our unique flight pattern. Some have hindered our journey for a Moment, but we recover and fly again. Attitude has

more to do with wing health then altitude!

❖ Every friend of each of my kids has touched my life. There are too many names and endless memories, birthdays, 16 surprise parties, proms, graduations...etc, etc... I LOVE YOU ALL!

❖ Camp Faithful has also brought so many friends. Willy's you are the friends everyone wishes they had. Kelly ...love you, you quiet angel you! Jackie...an angel for our family, thanks for flyin' to us! Kathy my Friday angel.. love you! Gramma...Angel for my Bim. Love you Bert! Daniel...I thank God for uniting you with my boys. Music angel that you are, wings flappin' strong for JC...I LOVE THAT! Zack and Christy...I pray always. All the angels who've encouraged the band and their love for the Lord...I LOVE THAT! Sheri...you will always be a sister, love you. Mrs Church...you're an angel. Boop...XXOO.

❖ Other angels I have been working on for years, I have to let go. My family has been bruised to the soul by our church. Beaten down by finances and stomped on by people we truly thought were friends.

My friend Nancy used to get so annoyed with me all the time 'cuz she thought I

was always happy, so she called me the "blue bird of happiness". Now Nanc, my buddy, I used to always call her my Tornado.

This friendship began 26 years ago. Blurred a bit by drugs and alcohol, but we're like sisters. My Tornado Angel is there when I need her and I've always been there for her. My youngest son Matthew and her Kristopher are 7 months apart in age.

One day not long ago I'm talking to my Boo about Jayla's first Birthday party. He says, "The Tornado says he's coming but we won't know until he's here." So I say, "The, what?" We laughed so hard. Neither of us knew that I called Nanc the Tornado and my kids call her son the Tornado.

My Tornado girl is slowing down a bit. Her son the Tornado is beginning his grown up storm 'cuz he's now 21.

As I mentioned all flyers are unique to their flight. There are many memories of tough tearful travels and gentle joyful journeys.

While camping with my family when the kids were little, Kimber and I were in the bathroom. A voice said, "You look just like somebody I know." I was in a stall and Kimberly was by the sink. I said, "Barb?" She said, "Buzz?" She could not believe how much Kimberly looked like me. We have helped each other fly, but for

me...well, she knows. Flying with Birdie, memories we share, unbreakable sisterhood. When we were younger our getting old dream has always been rocking on a porch together, smoking a joint (again okay to laugh).

John the Cook helped our whole family fly. My kids' vacation memories would be mostly with John at his cottage. We cherish those times that could fill another book. John never had children so mine became as important to him as he was to them. Being a food, cottage vacation, gift giving, super hero angel for us. Watching him lose his Mom, sister and brother, we tried to be his angels.

John adopted a yellow lab named Patches. This was his son. On his birthday he got fillet mignon. Years went by and John became sickly. We would babysit Patches for him. This went on for a long time. Not long after he asked us to take Patches for a time. He called one night and asked me to take Patches home for a visit. Two days later our family went to the beach and came home to a ringing phone. Douglas answered it, thank God. John was gone, with Patches by his side when they found him.

John has told us that he wanted to be cremated and his ashes spread on Salt Island near his cottage. Douglas and I, John's nephew and niece took our boat to Salt Island with John. As Douglas begins to sprinkle his angel, the wind is blowing and John got the last laugh. Douglas starts to spit because pieces of John are blowing into his mouth! He could make us laugh even when he was gone...I LOVE THAT! I am looking forward to seeing him again someday!

Angels don't fall from the sky...they emerge from within.

Brian, the boy I never had sex with, if you remember, took his own life. I had seen him the week before that. We got high together and he asked, like always, "Does Doug make you happy?" He was always concerned about me. He was a fellow flyer that I missed. I hope I get to see him someday.

My customers are also a part of my family. One of my very favorite customers followed me for thirty years, Margarite; she died the month after I came home from the hospital. I miss her.

My customer Pauline is 95 years old and one of my very favorite people. Pauline lost her husband at 45 and never married again. She tells me marriage is forever. She also lost her one and only daughter after going in for a simple surgery; she never came home. Talking to each other over the years, we find out her daughter and I have the same birthday. So we become angels for each other. Even at 95 my Pauline still flies.

This is something my Pauline gave me; it bonded us together as angels and I'll share it with all my angels:

I said, "God, I hurt"
God said, "That's why I gave you tears"
I said, "God, I'm depressed"

God said, "That's why I gave you sunshine"
I said, "God, life is so hard"
God said, "That's why I gave you loved ones"
I said, "God my loved one died"
God said, "So did mine"
I said, "God, it's such a loss"
God said, "Mine was nailed to a cross"
I said, "God, but your loved one lives",
God said, "So does yours"
I said, "God, where are they?"
God said, "Mine is on my right, yours is in the light"
I said, "God, it hurts"
God said, "I know child, I know"

TBI
(Traumatic Brain Injury)

One year ago today, August 12, 2007 (seems like 20), a motorcycle accident changed my life in an Moment!

I don't remember what happened but, they tell me I was "life-star"-red to Yale New Haven Hospital. I had a seizure, and was placed in a drug-induced coma. My first memory was the room spinning. People were at the foot of the bed and my husband was at the side of my bed holding my hand. There was a big tube in my mouth and everyone was crying. All I could think was, "I'm dying".

The next memory I have is being put in, what I thought was a truck (ambulance) to be taken to I didn't know where (Rehab Center). This was to be my new home for recovery. I could see cars out the window coming at me and I was scared to death. They put me in a wheelchair and I remember asking the lady to cut my head off 'cuz the pounding was so loud. Then and for a long time, I thought people

184

could hear the pounding in my head, but now I know they couldn't then and they can't.

This Rehab Center is where I learned to walk again. It sounds so easy, but I promise you, it's not. I had fractured my C1 vertebrae, my cranium was fractured in two places, and the sphenoid bone between my eyes had broken with the bounce of my brain. The staff explained it to me as a boxer's injury with years of being punched in the head. The resulting was a traumatic brain injury.

In the same accident Douglas had broken ribs, punctured a lung and dislocated his shoulder. The kids took turns sleeping with Daddy and the Lord sent other angels to help too. Thank you all.

The Rehab Center is where I met an angel that didn't appear to be one. His name was Tony. We were both in wheelchairs at first and they told us that we may not walk again, but that we had to try. We looked at each other and Tony said to me, "We are walking out of here right?" And I said, "We have to have faith". And he said, "You sound like my Mom".

We did some therapy that day and then we both went outside in our wheelchairs. Tony asked me if I wanted a cigarette. Not remembering that I had quit for nine years I said, "Yeah, why not?" My husband came to visit me about that time. His first reaction to the cigarette was, "You better not let the kids see you smoking". He explained to me that after twenty years of heavy smoking, I had quit. Then, after my Daddy died, I had chosen what I thought was the least of many evils and started smoking again. Douglas told me that I had been hiding that from my kids.

Of course they ended up finding out. I can't change it. God brings wisdom through much suffering. He will bring out into the light what is hidden in darkness whether you want Him to or not. Sometimes it destroys relationships, breaks hearts. Prayerfully I've learned that broken hearts are God's business.

I have let my children down since the accident. I feel I'm not what my children want me to be. Heck, I'm not what I want me to be. I've lived my life trying to protect my children from anything I thought might hurt them. When my smoking in secret came out and they

186

were all astounded and disgusted with me, I felt it mostly with my Kimberly. All I can say is I'm so sorry my angels.

Another strong memory of that time is my husband crying next to my bed. I asked him what was wrong. He looked at me and said, "I can't be the Mommy". Leah had been married three months before the accident and her husband was in the Navy. He was stationed in Florida at the time of the accident, so she had come home to see if I was going to live or die, and help her Daddy. Holding my hand crying, my husband told me that Leah's husband didn't turn out to be who we had all thought he was. Now Leah was pregnant, very sick from stress and had lost weight from her already small frame. Add to all that her worry of Mommy and Daddy. A year later my granddaughter, Jayla, is four months old and her birth father has never seen her. Jayla is an angel God sent to our family to help us through this fiery trial. I pray continually for her father.

My larger-than-life angel would have to be the man I married. We were both diagnosed with post-traumatic stress disorder after the accident. I went through a fire with my husband, flames I didn't see coming. As I recover, I guess I should have. He doesn't always make good choices, but like me it's 'cuz he's human.

Now, I can say I never knew how much I loved Douglas until this year. There is a plan for us. I'm not saying it's easy to believe when you're in the fire of the trial. As I am trying to fly, I have confidence in the truth of Love

I hold on angels to the fact that things happen for a reason on our trip of life. God speaks clearly in his word that he loves me just the way I am. People let us down; hurt us, reject us, and hate us. We must try to fly knowing that hurt, rejection and hate were things God's one and only Son went through for us. Love will lift us up to fly high when we give it all we got.

So angels, try to fly as if no one is watching, but know that He is... because He Loves You "Just the Way You Are".

Carefully fly on with me...

PTSD SPLASHES

(Still) One year post accident

God's mercy has been with me always as we travel on this trip of mine. I fly carefully so as not to crash land today. It's only because of His Amazing Grace that I'm still flying at all. This writing is a work of God.

My 4 angels see Mommy different now 'cuz I am. I'm trying to fly, but my wings are tired. I never used to let that show...ever. Now I can't help it. But, remembering what I've already flown through, and what I've learned along the journey, I know my wings will weather the storm, as will yours angels.

A year ago, at the end of this month was the darkest time of my life. Now, sitting in my room listening to my littlest angel Jayla, asleep on my bed, my cup overflows with joy. Her Mommy, my Leah, didn't sleep much last night because the baby didn't. I remember those days. So we'll fly through the "**now**".

My oldest son is planning his wedding. My youngest son was asked to play the drums for the church we are now attending. My oldest daughter will probably be divorced soon, try to start her life yet again. My youngest daughter is in Maine with Billy and Cathy for Grace's second birthday and to see her Jon. My children are growing up to have good character and are becoming very strong adults. This brings a healing to my wings.

Life is a trip and as I've traveled through uncharted territory sometimes it's been with only my angel voice inside. This gentle voice helped me on my journey to forgive others and especially myself. The ways I have been taught these lessons I wouldn't wish on anyone. But, obviously it's the only way I would hear the voice and use the lesson to help someone else fly.

One and a half years post-accident

Since the accident one and a half years ago, life is good. Drastically different, but good.

My friends are a much smaller group then I thought they would be, but they are true angels who will fly by my side or pull me up when I just can't fly. I LOVE THAT! I'm used to being the helper angel, not the one who needs help. This season of travel needing help to fly helps me to understand myself trying to always help others. Loving someone lifts your wings, being loved strengthens them. Now I know if I wasn't created that way, I'd be crying half the time.

So, Angels is your cup half full or half empty? My Douglas often has a half empty cup and the half that is full can get really angry. My cup is usually full. We even each other out. I'd say over this last year and a half for the first time that I can remember both our cups have Moments of complete emptiness. By nature we are both passionate people. We do whatever we do passionately. The physical pain and the confusion in my head, multiplied by circumstance in this part of my journey, has tattered my wings. Traveling on the path that I've chosen to follow, my goal has been to finish writing by the time I'm fifty. That's now three months away.

It has been quite a year and a half. Sometimes keeping even my smallest grain of sanity I must believe God has a plan. I would like to share with you one of my favorite quotes from Billy Graham:

"Sometimes the burdens of life weaken us. But to strengthen us we believe Jesus Christ will meet us at the end of our life's journey

and still love us, and that makes all the difference."

Journey on and remember with me why I am who I am!

As I'm writing tonight it's almost Valentine's Day. All my kids are here with three young men and their girls. Billy and Cathy are here from Maine to see his brother Mat before he goes to Iraq with the Marines. Aaron, their brother, his new wife who I don't really know yet, and Mat and Emily are also here. Emily will be waiting for her fiancé to come home from Iraq to be married. These three boys have been a large part of my journey. We met at our second church and they became part of our extended family. Mat, being the youngest of the three is my Matthew's best buddy since they were young. One of the changes in me now, is the fact I'm upstairs writing and listening. Feeling the excitement of them all being together for the first time in a long time, I used to be down there with them.

Now we jump a week ahead to Maine. My boys' band, the U.N.I.T.E.D, had a concert at

Brian's church. Brian is a young man we also met at our second church and is one of my oldest son's closest friends. With that you become part of my family. Brian met his wife Meghan while attending Christian college. They now have a daughter Ava and a son Seth. I praise God for young families like these that people never hear about. This weekend at the church in Maine is an awesome time for young people who love God or for young people who need to know that God loves them. I sometimes wonder what my life would have been if I had events like this to attend. But, that wasn't God's plan for my trip.

One week later, my Leah and Jackie, another extended family member, are at a Christian retreat for young adults. I'm excited 'cuz Jayla, my littlest angel is home with us. I LOVE THAT! Talking to Leah who misses her baby so much, she's having a wonderful time of laying her burdens down. The Lord tells us to give him our "junk" but it's not always easy. This struggle of life is very unique to each of us. Sometimes hearing another struggle helps.

I can say looking into our Jayla's eyes, I see pure joy when she's laughing, and pure dependency when she cries. That's why I think the sermon I heard on this particular Sunday, from the book of Matthew, was perfect. Matthew 18:1-4 "Disciples ask, 'Who is greatest in heaven?' Jesus called a child unto him and he said 'Except you become as little children, you will not enter into the kingdom of heaven. Who shall humble himself as this little child is greatest in the kingdom of heaven.' He didn't say "baby", He didn't say "teenager", He didn't say "adult", He said little children.   I'm such a lover of kids of any age. You can reach them and teach them the younger they are, a bit easier because they listen and do. I believe that's why He says little children, not older children, because the older we get, through our ups and downs the tougher we become, and the more stubborn and selfish we become. Jesus knows us! He is teaching us how to be adopted into His Father's family. I LOVE THAT!

Mat, the little Marine, has now left for Iraq. My Scotty has graduated high school, David has left the house. DJ got engaged, Jayla was born and the whole family was there...I LOVE THAT!

Ok, so other things in the year and a half- a confused divorce of a family we love, my buddy Ellen's husband left her as she had battled with cancer, Eddie went to prison, my brother in law Stevie got married to a woman we've never met. My son's band lost a bass player due to the world and gained one that is definitely U.N.I.T.E.D. They are recording their second CD. And my Kimberly has been blessed for living her life for Jesus with a boyfriend who lives the same. I LOVE THAT! A friend I thought of as a daughter betrayed me and broke my heart.

The terrain of our travel changes, from rocky, to bumpy, to smooth and back again. Whatever path we choose has a specific quality of beautiful scenery or nightmarish darkness.

So angels, try to have a little kid heart, being dependent only on our Creator. Easy for me to say now, I guess. After living through the last year and ½, I have been on the darkest ride of my trip. The only one who never left, always understood through the dark tunnels, listened to my screams and loved me still, was Jesus.

Two years post-accident

Its 8 days to my 2-year celebration of being alive. God didn't punch his time clock for me, just slowed me down to listen better. I haven't always been thankful for every day of my last two years, although I have learned from them.

I just found out my old friend Jody's Dad passed away. My heart breaks for Daddy's little girl cause I know how she feels. Loss is not a trip any of us like to take. Thinking of him brings back lots of happy memories as he was a very cool guy; he will be missed.

As I continue to travel, the blessings unfold. Watching the U.N.I.T.E.D play at the largest Christian music festival in New England can only be compared to one thing: the birth of my first grandchild. Seeing them perform on the jumbo TV screen in front of so-so many people was indescribable. I was overwhelmed watching my baby on drums, my oldest singing and playing guitar.

When DJ started playing his guitar, I flashed back to him at age 4 on the edge of the bathtub with his first Christmas guitar. I went in, sat on the toilet, and asked him why he was in the bathroom. My 4 year old immediately answered, "I'm practicing". I asked him what he was practicing for, and he answered, "So I be good".

All the practicing was planning for this day. AND I'm alive to fly with them...I LOVE THAT!

Before we went to New Hampshire for Soulfest, Douglas got a phone call. It was an offer to buy our property next door which was not up for sale. He discussed it, and told the guy what he wanted. A few back and forth phone calls and SOLD! For exactly what he asked. The family that lives there can't really afford to live there. We agreed to wait until there was a closing date to talk to Jen. While I was babysitting Gracie yesterday she told me she didn't want to move. I will miss Taylor and Grace, but we have to make our life simple. Douglas and I have taken care of so many people over the years our wings are tattered and tired. The offer for our property came directly from God...I LOVE THAT!

Jayla said "Bobci" really clear for the first time today which is "Grandma" in Polish...I LOVE THAT!

Kimberly has been voted in to Camp Faithful as the Youth Committee Chairperson. The blessing for my Kimber is ...wind under her wings. Everyone deserves appreciation for a job well done. She put her heart into this endeavor and God says, "Fly upward angel." I LOVE THAT!

Our family is looking forward to the Sept 18th 2009 wedding of DJ and Molly. Becoming a husband, homeowner, and all that entails is exciting and frightening, especially when you've had a father like my larger than life angel, Douglas.

By nature, as I find out who I am myself, I am not a control freak, never have been. My Douglas however by nature IS. Douglas has always struggled with allowing his children to learn life on their own. It's rough for him. When they get hurt he tries with all his might to protect. Case in point...Leah marrying a boy her Daddy begged her not to. But he is so in love with our family's littlest angel, Jayla, and she with him and it's taught him they will get hurt. Jayla is the blessing that the Lord had for our little Leah. I continue to learn we are not in control! Our kids were very small when we started explaining that Daddy is the Captain and Mommy is the Co-Captain. Our family has always been a team I guess. All four of them never had to wonder if their Captain would take care of them...I LOVE THAT! I believe angels, that this is why, after all our team has been through, that the six of us still trust God our Father and believe on Jesus our Best Friend...I LOVE THAT!

The U.N.I.T.E.D went to West Virginia on a mission trip the day after Soulfest. They met a lot of people. Splitting up into teams, they were not all together yet together blessed. It was a wonderful time of serving the Lord, we all missed them.

Just two days ago was my old friend Jody's birthday. I was in prayer 'cuz losing your Dad is just suck. That same day Billy & Cathy had Meghan, Gracie's new little sister on their 6th wedding anniversary.

These last two years have changed me, grown me. My wings are stronger in some ways, much weaker in others.

God works in ways we don't understand, we can't. Never knowing what He has in store is part of the excitement of flight. No matter how much planning we do, only God truly knows our path from beginning to end...I LOVE THAT! Some people are frustrated by that but for me, it is a comfort.

Tomorrow I celebrate two years of new life. None of our trips are easy. Try to laugh a lot, especially at yourself. Laughing has always helped me fly. Crying usually weighs me down. I fold my tattered, tired wings and I pray for all of you to be encouraged so you can encourage someone who needs you. You're thinking, "How do you know I'm loved?" My angels, God told me. I LOVE YOU for sharing my flight. So, dust your wings, laugh and help someone to fly!

Hebrews 13:2 "Don't forget to be concerned about strangers, for by doing this, some people have shown concern to *angels* without knowing it."

My oldest son's wedding was definitely the most romantic one I've ever attended. When DJ saw his Molly coming towards him in a horse and carriage he began to cry. The closer she got the harder he cried. After all, marriage is an extreme part of our journey. He's found the other half of himself and his love is profound.

They were married by a young man named Mikey, who we've known for years and my family adores. It was the first wedding he's ever done. His words had much wisdom and love. With our church issues he was perfectly picked by God.

I could go on and on about this most beautiful day, the weather, tears of joy and so on. But, when this young couple danced their first dance, "I Can't Help Falling in Love With You", by Elvis, OH MY! DJ recorded himself singing for his love. Later through Katie, Molly's sister, we all learned that this was the first song he ever sang to her; that's my boy!

Before my son was to be married, I called Terry to ask her for a ride to the pawn shop. I wanted to do something special for my first-born. I sold my chain, charms, and some of my Mom's jewelry and I could do it! Saving money from the few customers I have, Terry brought me to make payments. I wanted my son to love his rehearsal dinner. Molly's parents were giving their daughter a beautiful wedding in Connecticut from far away California. I've never done anything like that without Douglas and it felt great! That's One of my best memories for my boy not to be embarrassed...I LOVE THAT

My Molly Nell is due in June with their first baby. I can't wait!

Fast forward to Oct 6, 2009, our 30th wedding anniversary; that's right! 30 stinkin' years! WOW, what a trip it's been! We renew our vows every 10 years. Before we were married we knew in ten years we would be different but we never realized how much you can change in ten year. The changes in life over ten years are incredible. So that was our agreement, every ten years.   Well, this time I didn't care. Our kids were beginning their adult traveling; it's their turn.

By now I've planned three weddings for us. My original gown changed a bit each time. Ten years ago I covered the lace with motorcycle grease, twenty added pearls. Approaching 30 years I threw it away, but my larger than life angel took it out of the garbage and had it cleaned. I still can't believe it didn't fall apart! However it stayed together; very symbolic of *us*! Jesus took us out of the garbage and changed a few things. Sometimes we go back to garbage, but we haven't fallen apart yet, just like my gown! Interestingly it still fits, like we fit each other.

My kids took over this plan of our renewing, mostly my Kimberly. A luau to remember forever. Our first dance is always the same, Billy Joel's "I LOVE YOU JUST THE WAY YOU ARE". Still the perfect song for us!

We have enjoyed life no matter what season we're in. Our first honeymoon was in the 70's, so the Poconos it was. A very drunken season but we met Gary and Sue and had a blast. Ten years later with four kids, and saved by grace we went to Niagara Falls. For twenty years, Douglas surprised me with a cruise...AWESOME! Every time we did something we'd never done before. At thirty years we went to CAPE COD. We met a lesbian couple and enjoyed our anniversary dinner with them; that night, again, a first!

So angels, this journey continues because God hasn't chosen to call us home. We've had some close calls, but still here.

One thing I've learned, angels beyond all else is this...you need to learn to fly in the rain and this is why...if we only had sunny travels we'd be a desert-DRY. We need the storms of life to teach us. Through these fifty years of bumps and bruises, I have thought of myself as a helper. The wisdom I cherish now is we ALL have storms...and we ALL need help flying through them. All of us, no matter how different we are, have storms that change our flight. Don't laugh at other angel's storms, HELP THEM. Comfort each other through Jesus Christ. Our storms produce patient endurance.

Three years post-accident

Today, August 12, 2010, I celebrate the third year of grace filled travel. My second grandchild was born July 3, with all of us in the waiting room. His name is Dublin James.

He's beautiful. Before that, on June 10th the Thursday following my Molly's baby shower, she lost her Mom. Our hearts broke for our Molly. Her parents live in California which made it more difficult. Today Molly and Dublin flew to Cali. My son will join his wife and son for a memorial service.

Life is fragile angels. A Moment can change all flight. It's been said, "You never know what you have until it's gone"...don't wait.

This is grandparent season and it is unspeakably joyful...I LOVE THAT!

One smile can change one life

One hug can change one day

Encouragement can lift hurt

Laugh because even a baby understands

Lending an ear of compassion changes sorrow

Take a Moment...

Smile *Hug*
Encourage*Laugh*Listen...Be
an Angel

VA-KLEMPT...

(Otherwise known as Verklempt)

One Moment that I can't remember changed me. I'm flying through recovery, menopause and extreme change inside and out. I can't smell or taste, but I can walk. I don't always say the right words, but I can talk. My headache is a constant but I try to laugh more then I cry.

As we fly through our journey we don't remember years, months or days. What us earth angels remember are Moments. Our trip of life is made up of Moments that guide our flight. Angels cherish your Moments.

Last week my Leah, through her divorce became a Malinowski again. It's a new season for her and her little girl. In 2011, enter Seth, Hailey, and Seth Jr. Thank God for a class for single mothers that God used to bring Seth into our family. Leah, I told you he would come. The Lord declares your hope for the future!!!!! XO

My Kimber is in love and moving to New Hampshire for a season.

My DJ is going to be a Daddy again.

My Matthew is looking forward to finishing the band's third CD and playing at Soulfest again.

I just found the photo album where I pressed the rose my larger than life angel gave me with a pearl ring. Funny, how memories can change one Moment into giggles or tears.

Watching my children's paths change into their own adult character leads into other memories.

At Christmas-time Douglas and I could never let go of leaving cookies and watching little faces when they were gone. I believe we balanced the birth of our Savior and Mr and Mrs Claus well. The sacrifices of no sleep made were always worth the faces of my four angels.

The best gift for Molly this year was her Dad and brother came from Cali and surprised her...I LOVE THAT!

This season is adjusting to unknown travel. Angels, that's faith. It is the substance of things hoped for and the evidence of things unseen. I LOVE THAT...When you're at a loss for words, as you will be through your trip, you are Va-klempt.

Today I write to you on January 12, 2011. It's been three years and five months and I'm still flying.

A memory I have that I love is finding a picture for my DJ. It's him with an old Elvis-type microphone and it reads, "Music is what feelings sound like"; so true. My son doesn't realize how strong an angel he's been for me. An incredible portion of my journey has been watching his flight.

Here in Connecticut we have 20 inches of snow. Kimber, Leah and Jayla are out playing in it. DJ, Tank, Daniel, and Zack are still in the process of recording the third U.N.I.T.E.D. CD. I stand Va-klempt.

Little Cathy, an angel who's flight is awesome to be a part of, had a loss. Her boy, Bandit, the best dog, passed on. Barb, my safe place angel, misses her Max. Two women in very different seasons of life resemble the same pain. Moments come that we wish could miss us...they don't ...**BAM**...Change of flight.

As my trip of life rolls on I am convinced that faith becomes wings for prayer. I know my flight has been prepared just for me and yours for you. A snowflake always reminds me how unique we are. We just had a huge snowstorm; millions of flakes, each unique. Just like us...I LOVE THAT!

My friends are still fewer than I thought they would be. Since we had been saved by grace, church members have been our family, but no more. A very difficult part of flying through life is loss.

Mother Theresa said, "A joyful heart is the result of a heart burning with love." This is how I explain why I can be joyful through dark lonely travel; 'cuz my heart burns with love for so many. I am Va-klempt to express how easily your heart can break. Broken hearts need to be loved back together. I believe in love even when I don't feel loved. I believe in sunshine even when it's dark. As I sit here memories of unbearable pain, unbelievable joy, I stand Va-klempt.

I got a plaque for Christmas which says, "Life takes us to unexpected places, Love brings us home". Billy and Cathy...I LOVE THAT!

On December 11, Douglas' birthday, Tina passed on. Tina was in her 40s. On January 11, we got a call from my father-in-law, his wife has passed on. Vi was in her 70s. Each had one daughter and one son. Once again, two extremely different women in different stages of their journey. Their connection? Douglas and I. It's a small world angels, we're all connected through common ground.

Look in the mirror, angels, you are living proof miracles happen. Even in my crazy stupid times I've been given grace. The reason I can forgive much is I have been forgiven much on my flight. Being forgiven helps your heart, forgiving others gives it wings, forgiving yourself sets you free.

We need awful valleys to appreciate the high places we fly to. Faith makes our flight possible...**NOT EASY!** But, fly we must.

This next event brings more memories. It's a Saturday. I began it with Jayla's face to mine, "You up Bochi?" That's a perfect way to start my day. My customer, Marion wanted a color. Then I had therapy with Patti (Thank You XO). It was raining which always makes my head loud and more painful. Shirley, my mother-in-law calls; her mother has passed on. After therapy and coloring Marion's hair we go to my brother-in-law Eddie's celebration of his 50th birthday. We go to "The Office", a hometown bar like Cheers back in the day, right Birdie? From there we go to the funeral home to view Nana. My buddy Ellen is with us cause she's with Eddie. (Never could I have predicted *this* situation.) During this full day of memories, Nancy calls. She asks if we knew anybody who would want free tickets to Billy Ray Cyrus. Va-klempt I say, "Yeah, let's go". Heavily medicated, in the tenth row he begins to sing "Amazing Grace"...I LOVE THAT! This day of ups, down, and everything in between, means more memories.

My mother-in-law is now seriously ill with pneumonia. I'm in much prayer for Shirley. So many memories I can't pick one...I love you.

As I pick up my notebook to write today, as always I read what I wrote last. I can't write today. I will get with you soon angels.

I'm back. My mother-in-law has left us for the streets of gold a few weeks after her Mom. She was the toughest little broad I've ever known. Watching her three boys try to take this shock with their mother's courage is hard to watch.

We buried Shirley a day before Mother's Day. You can't make this stuff up. This Mother's Day in church was rough. Usually you get a flower or something. This time, the gift was a key chain with a flashlight from Women of Faith. Shirley had accepted Christ at a Women of Faith Conference. It felt as if God was clearly telling me, "She's okay". Then, in church, on Mother's Day, the pastor sings a song I have never heard sung in church, "Teach Your Children Well" by Crosby, Stills and Nash. Now, I have been to only one concert with Shirley in the thirty plus years I've known Shirley; that's right angels: Crosby, Stills and Nash! I miss you Shirley Mae, but God helped my heart. Thank you Jesus...I LOVE THAT!

For this Moment angels I'm doing the best I can to touch you gently with my broken wings. "Sometimes things can't be seen or even touched; they must be felt with the heart" in the words of Helen Keller. For me that explains grace and love.

On the 22 of May my Terry lost her second sister. Gail loved daisies so Terry was hunting. I was going to help her do the picture boards for the wake. In the last place we stopped to look for daisies I asked her to get me a big Red Bull. Terry goes to the back of the car to put the daisies she found in the trunk and says to me, "I hope this is big enough." I turned to look. She is holding a huge red bow and I'm thinking, "Why would she get that for Gail's wake?" But what I said was, "Yeah, that's big enough". I'm still thinking, "Why the big red bow?" when it hits me and I begin to laugh. She says, "Why are you laughing?" I say, "I wanted a big red *bull*!"...I LOVE THAT! All I wanted that day was to lift Terry and help her fly through this day. Sometimes, the difference between an ordinary day and an extraordinary day is just a little extra. That bow is getting cut in half and framed for each of us. We made a terrible day better with a red bow laugh.

I'm leaving you angels Va-klempt as I am... one more memory.

My larger than life angel had a patch sewn on his hat. It was a Harley Davidson symbol and behind it were broken wings. He got it to represent his broken heart for his Mom. He told the sewing woman his reason and she asked if he knew what broken wings behind Harley really meant. He didn't. She told him, "It represents a bike crash". Now his broken wings have a double meaning for him.

Don't worry about making a mess because those are memories in the making.

STILL TRIPPIN'

Four years post-accident

In the four years and seven months since the accident, as they must, things have changed. Since we've been together angels I've had four more grandchildren. I've gotta' say my kids make beautiful babies!

My prodigal angel is moving to Camp Faithful beginning her new life as Wife, Mom and Step-Mom. What Seth and Leah have taken on in one year seems too too much. But, angels our flights are unique and my little Leah flies fast. Their Logan Douglas, our newest edition is nine days old today. His sister Jayla loves her baby. Seth Jr and Haylie are excited for their new little brother too.

Brody Davis is DJ and Molly's second son and he is three months old today. He was born on my larger than life angel's birthday.

My heart jumps for joy 'cuz I watched both Logan and Brody be born...I LOVE THAT!

It's now **February 29th, 2012, leap** year...OH MY. Just what I need; **an extra day.** So, I take the extra and add it to the ordinary, 'cuz I have to, to be able to fly.

In these last few months I have given my oldest son and my oldest daughter their baby books and their tubs of treasures. I always felt it was very important that my children would be able to look back to their beginnings. As I gave DJ and Leah their stuff the Moment was more emotional for me then my Angels. I LOVED IT.

I know, angels that writing in baby books is a tad obsessive when your babies are in their twenties. However, as you will remember I don't balance well. Now that I'm older I know why I have done this; I don't have any history. I only have questions that will never be answered. From me, my children will never have to ask.

I am still writing in Kimberly and Matthew's baby books. My **boo** wants to know when he can have his. Apparently, the way you get your stuff is when you have a family of your own. Because then I just make another chapter to my book. Write I must.

My son's band has been **through flight changes.** Another Christian band who has more money and support contacted DJ to possibly bring legal action over the name "The U.N.I.T.E.D." Since my son is NOT a fighter, his band is now "Waking Unity".

THE LOVE MOVEMENT, Waking Unity's first CD, speaks to our battle in this trip of life. Two members of the band have left, and one was replaced immediately by divine appointment. As a "Band Mom" the last song of this incredible CD is VICTORY!

I pray as I watch my sons battle with their flight patterns. I hold on with them as they fly with demons unseen, and I will jump with them in their victory.

Seasons change as they must and bring us to who we will become.

Today I brought the last of the one hundred books I ordered in excitement, to Bonnie who works at my hair supply store. I get there as she's walking out the door. **She starts running to me. We share a huge hug, MY SISTER!** She says "I read your book. **My daughter is adopted, and we have shared similar paths.**" That's right; **I had already given** Bonnie a book...and forgot.

That's TBI (**traumatic brain injury**); invisible to others but we can't wear a sign. It's **a battle fought for me through faith also unseen. So the last book I ended up brining to** my friend Lois. She's in the hospital with **a virus that affected her brain, so we had plenty to talk about: confusion, frustration, and fear. Unfortunately, I understand completely. How you face a battle builds strength in your wings to help someone else fly...I LOVE THAT!**

Saturday, May 13, Waking Unity had a concert we had planned to go to. That afternoon DJ calls and tells Douglas, "We **showed up and no one knows about the concert. Dad, could we play in the back yard tonight?**" Of course!

DJ and Tank have gotten to know another young man named Ray, with an **awesome testimony.** Ray started a ministry to reach, teach and love the un-lovables. He came up with a t-shirt business called "Grateful Apparel" to fund this ministry. These young men had united to present "The Grateful Tour".

Ray came to our back yard from New York. Waking Unity came home and gave their all. A beautiful thing was happening, then the cops came. Even my larger than life, Correction Officer husband with a badge couldn't fix this. We just laugh!

Next day, Mother's Day, Molly, Kimber, and Leah take me aside to tell me, they got me a surprise next weekend for my birthday. I love surprises! After each of them telling me the other was pregnant...NOT the surprise. They had gotten us a room which was 20 minutes from the band's next concert...I LOVE THAT!

My birthday comes on Friday. Birdie and I go to the movies. That was a perfect time for us. Saturday, I do Marion's hair, then Jenna's for her prom. I had done Jenna's mom Paula's hair for her prom and then wedding. Second generation...I LOVE THAT!

Douglas was working at Camp Faithful that day and comes home all excited. It's a beautiful day and he's decided to take the bike out for our trip to my room present. I know real panic while getting my crazy brain wrapped around motorcycle birthday journey. Alas, I go with the flow 'cuz if he's happy, then I'm happy.

This is not a relationship for everyone; this one is uniquely mine. Loving my Douglas means riding the ups, downs, zigs and zags together. So I had the mindset of car travel turn into...BAM...biker birthday.

This bed and breakfast, Susan's sanctuary, was definitely where we were to be. It was possibly the most comfortable and peaceful I've been in 4 years and nine months (that's how long it's now been since my life changing Moment). I met Susan. She and I are about the same age, so I have a new friend...I LOVE THAT!

My angels, when the first prints of my book came I gave one to each of my children. I asked Douglas to read it, but being the Douglas he is, he said, "No, I lived it". His choice, yet I lived it. I believe this is the one and only thing I have ever done just for me. Also for you angels, 'cuz all of us have our battles. Help each other fly. If you can laugh at yourself it's easier to fly.

On August 12, 2012 I will be celebrating 5 years of a trip that could have ended in a Moment. My God saw fit to bless me with a change in flight pattern.

One more quote, this time from Abraham Lincoln:

"It's not the years in your life, it's the life in your years." I LOVE THAT!

Fly on...almost there

Hey, my angels! Today is four years and eleven months since God gave me another try at my trip.

Yesterday, July 11, 2012, my friend Lois went to sleep to wake with Jesus. Her painful struggle is done...HALLELUJAH!

Last night I HAD to see my brother Arthur. Lately, he has been on my heart so heavy sometimes it's difficult to fly, but things happen, flight changes and I hadn't gone. Last night I HAD to. The passing of Lois yanked my heart to go and I finally listened. I thank my God for his current wife, Blanca. I'm also thankful for all the family that came with her; I love you all! My Bible says, "God will have mercy on whom He will have mercy." Angels, this is obviously not our decision who goes to heaven and who doesn't. Surviving Vietnam changed by big brother. Holding his hand in the last days of his journey, memories were rushing through my head.

He looked at me with his beautiful blue eyes and said, "Do you still want to marry me?" Now in a hospital bed with a morphine drip, I answer, "Yes." His eyes rolled back, he squeezes my hand and says, "I can't."

So, my friend Lois passed, God told me to go see my brother. So angels, try to listen before there's no time. Arthur knew who I was and I got to hold his hand and tell him how much I love him... Thank you Jesus! In the midst of all these emotions, my Birdie has gall bladder surgery. Wednesday, July 11, 2012 was a long draining Moment.

My Arthur passes on Sunday. Getting the call right after church, my heart is relieved; his pain is over. My friend Lois' wake is that night. I asked my larger than life, Douglas, not to tell anyone about Arthur because this night is supposed to be for Lois' family. But, my larger than life angel just *has* to. So, my hug to Mikey (the same man who married my DJ and Molly), who just lost his mom, went this way...As we hug, I tell Mikey, "She loved you SO much!" Mikey replies, "I'm so sorry for *you*." (REALLY DOUGLAS??!!!) Angels, I take a breath and adapt. Oh, this journey I'm on is anything but boring.

On July 13, 2012, my larger than life angel injured his knee at work. In the prison, when they call a Code for help, you just run. My man ran faster than his knee was willing to run.

Before the scheduled surgery on his knee, Douglas wanted to go see his brother, Eddie, who recently moved to Hollywood, Florida. Since I'd had a terribly emotional week, losing my friend and my last piece of family, I wanted to go too. Angels, it's always nice to know that some things, and some people, never change...that's my Eddie. We wanted to make sure that he was ok, and he was. In this journey we saw my father-in-law and his new live-in girl, Pam. He's happy, she's sweet. We saw extended family, Ma and Brian. Brian's daughter Alex is going to cosmetology school, like I did. I pray for her and love her. Douglas and I brought Alex and her boyfriend to feed some gators. You would have thought we'd brought them to Disney...priceless!

I almost forgot! Barbie and Amanda. These two are friends we met, through our trips to my brother's house when he lived in Daytona, Florida. Barbie just happened to be visiting her brother in New Jersey when my brother passed. We talked, they came, AWESOME. On our way to Florida to see Eddie, we brought Barbie and Amanda, her daughter, back to Jersey. Her brother's house is a mansion down the street from Bruce

Springsteen...what? Angels, you never know what is going to enter or leave your flight pattern. ..I LOVE THAT!

Angels, I'm going to say that some news we got on our way home from Florida is what I'm going to leave you with. The last time Douglas and I were in Hampton Beach, New Hampshire, I was praying. Nothing new, but listen, angels...there is outdoor shell stage where concerts are held. I was walking around all the seats, asking the Lord to hear my cry. My son needs encouragement in his heart and soul to know the gift of musical talent he has been given is rightly used. That day I was praying for my oldest and youngest to be playing here at Hampton Beach someday. (This is a place I grew up visiting. There was even a Buzzell's Taffy Store on the beach when I was young and because it was my last name, I had been sure it had something to do with my Daddy.) So on our way home from Florida, DJ calls and explains to Douglas that Waking Unity has been invited to play at the Hampton Beach Shell! "Are you kidding me Lord?" I ask. Sit down, angels...the date they are scheduled to play is Sunday, August 12, 2012, exactly five years to the day from Sunday, August 12, 2007, the date of our motorcycle accident. When I heard the news,

 "I started singing, singing in my soul!"

Five years post-accident

August 12, 2012. The angels who came to Hampton Beach New Hampshire that day are cherished more than they will ever know. Each have played a part in healing my broken wings. There is unspeakable joy in my heart and we had a crazy bike time...I LOVE THAT!

Two weeks later, Douglas has knee surgery. From upstairs I hear, "POOP!" He has been home three days...OH MY. He is doing well. A week after that, he developed two blood clots in his calf on the leg of the knee that was operated on. I remember the doctor told us it could happen to 1% of the knee surgeries he's performed. Leave it to Douglas to be the 1%! Eventful, as always.

Ok, angels this is it. Remember why I refer to you as angels; it's so I can pray for y'all. Writing has helped me tremendously in seeking myself. Many things were left out for the sake of others.

My trip of life has severely changed in my past five years of travel. It's like this, some of Poop-y is still here, some of that part of me was shattered. For the first time since I became a hairdresser in 1978, Douglas didn't renew my cosmetology license. Maybe it shouldn't affect me, but it does.

Another severe change is that I've always done what I wanted to do. Now, I can't always drive when I want to. This menopause season of life allows me to pray for younger female angels, that they will find a cure for it before this happens to them!

Another severe change is that I have a hard time crying. Maybe it's because I've cried enough, or maybe it's the medication given to me when I couldn't stop crying.

As I reflect on how God could love me, the Spirit brings me back to John 3:16. Angels, God didn't send His son to us because we were perfect; we wouldn't have needed Him. This Scripture verse explains how God loves me and all of you:

John 3:16 "For God so loved THE WORLD that He gave His only Son that whoever believes in Him will not perish, but have everlasting life."

Throughout the sharing of this journey of mine, I hope it's evident that I became a born-again Believer, at times taking small steps, and sometimes leaps, toward Jesus. Once I was just was a daughter-adopted daughter-granddaughter-addict-dropout-licensed hairdresser-people pleaser-wife-mother-saved by grace Christian-medical patient-SURVIVOR-FIGHTER-BOCHI-LOVER OF ALL ANGELS. Now, I am just a Child of God and that's all I ever have to be. When my feet hit the floor in the morning I want the devil to say, "OH CRAP SHE'S UP!"

Angels, angels what can I say, so many events in this trip of life. It's hard to have a last chapter 'cuz the journey continues!

As you have flown with me, I hope the flight stirred you either to travel lighter or to fly higher.

Make the most of even the smallest Moments of your trip. Hopefully, you will cherish the fact that every Moment is a big one, 'cuz those Moments make you who you are.

Proverbs 10:12 "**Love** covers all sins."